THE QUEENING OF CERIDWEN

THE QUEENING OF CERIDWEN

By

ESTHER ELIAS

Author Of
"Profile Of Glindy — A Welsh Corgi"

THE CHRISTOPHER PUBLISHING HOUSE
WEST HANOVER, MASSACHUSETTS
02339

PRINTED IN

THE UNITED STATES OF AMERICA

TO CERIDWEN

"Her ways are ways of pleasantness,
and all her paths are peace."
Proverbs 3-17

OVER THERE ....

Over there on that distant shore called Heaven are two dogs, Glindy and Ceridwen, waiting for their mistress to get there. It will be a great day, a joyful Reunion for the three of them when that day comes, as come it will at the end.

We talked often about Heaven, Ceridwen and I. It was a place where you went and never came back, I told her, and it helped to explain where Glindy was and why he wasn't with us anymore. I'd say, "He went to Heaven... *we'll* go there too some day...he's waiting for us...do you understand?"

She understood, my Ceridwen, about Heaven — earthly things, too — understanding being the very core of her being, her very "essence," you could say.

CONTENTS

"QUEENIE"

The first thing my brother said upon seeing the little four-months-old puppy from Wales, was: "What's her name?—I don't know what *you're* going to call her, but *I'm* going to call her 'Queenie,' for she looks like a little queen to me!"

He made it sound like an ultimatum, and all ears, her Ladyship liked this, and I did too, as I said: "Thank-you-sir for the compliment"—since she really *did* have a queenly bearing even at that early age.

Continuing the conversation, I answered: "Her name is Ceridwen, but I'm going to call her 'Cerid,' as in *did*. It's an old, familiar feminine name in Wales, immortalized in the Mabinogion Tales, and elsewhere in Welsh literature."

My brother kept quiet for he didn't care a hoot about Welsh literature, but I had given the name much thought on the plane going over to Wales to fetch her, and had been reading up on it in Welsh reference books at home and in our local Carnegie Library. Would she be like the Ceridwen in Taliesen's life, the famous Welsh bard, reputed by some to be the *author* of the Mabinogion Tales, and by others to be his mother Ceridwen, endowed with supernatural powers? Or perhaps she would more resemble one of the many guises in which the poet and author *Robert Graves* pictured her in his novel "The White Goddess"?

The discussion ended and little Miss Ceridwen soon settled down into his heart and mine. Later, when she grew up and had a family, some of the regal bearing disappeared from her body, but never from the way she held her head. In that respect, she was queenly, and like a goddess to the very end.

PART ONE

Chapter 1

IN THE BEGINNING

Let's get into a happy mood to write about Ceridwen, for though she suffered the last two years of her life, it is as a happy being we will always remember her. She enjoyed life and wanted everyone else to do the same; and resolutely projected the bright side of things into all she was and did. That was at the root of her playful ways to the last, and was the most outstanding feature of her character, that and her endless determination. Cheerfulness and determination, two wonderful traits for anyone and especially for a dog. These traits, along with her two "p's"—Patience and Perseverance—were the watchwords of her life.

Corgis are usually high-strung and nervous. Glindy, her mate and lifelong love was; and though his was the stronger character of the two, her character was strong, too—quietly strong, and serene. Nerves never were a problem with her. If something went wrong in our daily lives, she "accepted" for all three of us, without getting upset and though Glindy and I didn't always appreciate this quality those first years of our knowing her, it was there; and plain to be seen after he died.

I'll never forget the day I met her. It's more than 3,000 miles from Pittsburgh to Carmarthenshire, Wales, where Ceri, Cousin Tim's son, had promised to keep a puppy from his last litter of corgis for me. Tim had died and Ceri was now running Cross Hill Farm, at the crossroads between Llanfihangel Ar Arth, and Pencader. Not only a breeder of fine pedigreed corgis, Tim also had been a notable breeder of *all* farm animals, great and small, and particularly Hereford cattle. Would Ceri be an expert breeder like his father? Well, we were soon going to see. This was in August 1966 and little Miss Ceridwen, his selection, was as already mentioned, four months old.

Some six years earlier Tim had bred and sent me Glindy, as fine a corgi as ever lived, for a retirement present. Still without progeny, I wanted a mate for him to carry on his line—at that time it was the goal of my life—and I was going back to Wales to get one from the same farm where he had been born.

The minute I got to the farm after the long trying plane trip to London and the endless train ride down into Wales, I sized up the beautiful little red and white corgi Ceri had set aside, but delayed the actual confrontation until the next morning, since it was already dark and I was terribly tired from the journey.

Full of confidence from my years with Glindy and thinking there was nothing about a puppy I couldn't handle, we started for our walk the next day, but I saw that little Miss Ceridwen didn't want to go a-walking, though she had been playing with me all morning. Usually when I took Glindy for a walk he was so eager, it was a case of the cart pulling the horse, but it wasn't that way at all with Ceridwen. For after we got started and had gone a little way, nothing, no one could move her and she sat right down in the middle of the road in that bustling farm community, fully prepared to sit there forever. All the cows, cars, farmers, farmers's carts ambling along, yes even the passersby, had to detour around her, and what's more she was plainly enjoying herself and their predicament.

I used every wile at my command, but nothing worked. It wasn't plain cussedness, it wasn't even determination as such, it was just the disarming Welsh flair for being unswayed, and not liking to be rushed, this "Welshness." It was good to see, and the few misgivings I had been having on the plane coming over vanished immediately. This was *my* dog from that moment. I knew she would be Glindy's dog, too, and that we three were going to be a happy threesome, instead of the lonely pair Glindy and I had often been. It was an exciting prospect as it ran through my mind, when suddenly, and without any warning, she broke away from me and scooted down the road to the Cross Hill Farm gate, with half the village laughing its head off at the sight. And *there* she waited for me.

That was Ceridwen at four months of age and she was heartwarming to her Welsh-American companion who had always, all her life, been partial to things Welsh, and felt now everything about the little dog was going to turn out all right.

* * * * *

There hadn't been much of a life for her up to then because, generally speaking, Welsh farms and farmers are so overburdened with work there's not much time to spend with puppies—and puppies are for cuddling. Her mother, "Linda Lassie," looked after her as well as she could, but little Ceridwen was a frolicsome young one and needed attention every minute. The Cross Hill Farm folks were busy from morning till night with chores. Further, in breeding circles litters generally changed hands by weaning time and there was no point in becoming attached to puppies. Thus, the four-months-old puppy they had been keeping for me, was somewhat out of place at Cross Hill Farm.

Farm dogs are rarely quartered in the house in Wales. Most farm dogs live their whole lives outdoors, or in the barn with the other animals. Corgis have their work to do, too, like the other animals on the premises, they being used for rounding up herds of cows into or out of the barn, the way sheep dogs round up sheep. But little Ceridwen was too young to be useful.

By day she kept herself busy running about with her mother in the farmyard. At night she was housed in her own snug little doghouse near the barn, while Linda Lassie, her mother, was in an impregnable little stockade nearby, for she was a brood bitch and usually in whelp or in season, and had to be safely protected from neighboring male dogs.

So it was a lonely life. A large Alsatian dog belonging to the Farm was housed in the barn by day but at night was loosed for protection of the farm property, and slept in the yard. Lonely he was, too, with his only real chum a jovial old sow, who mothered him and indeed mothered all of them, and kept them company.

It was an odd "menagerie" and my arrival in their midst was a welcome diversion for all of them. I was given complete charge of the puppy and her mother and played with them most of the day, though I never took the mother dog away from the house for fear of meeting neighboring male dogs I couldn't cope with.

* * * * *

Llandysul and the First Days of My Stay

Now that Ceridwen and I were to have the whole fortnight in which to get acquainted before departing for America, we wasted no time in preliminaries but set right into behaving like old friends. Our first walk—when she had so determinedly squatted in the middle of the road and refused to move—had established an understanding between us and we never had such a confrontation again. She became more tractable and of course I had learned something, too—namely that compulsion was not the word for Ceridwen. Persuasion was the word, with a capital "P".

We were outdoors from sunup till sundown and the weather was favorable for the entire fortnight. Sometimes we would go up the road and sit in the fields with the cows. Sometimes we would walk down the road to the old churchyard where Cousin Tim, Ceri's father, was buried. I would read the epitaphs on the tombstones to her in my atrocious Welsh. All ears she was, though they didn't offer much interest to *me* being about Carmarthenshire folks, and I had had a Cardiganshire background. She seemed to be taking in everything I said and I talked incessantly, telling her about Glindy back home in America whom she was soon going to meet; that he, like she, had been born at Cross Hill Farm and all the other things a puppy and her mistress talk about.

Other times we would go inside old St. Michael's Church to explore. Ceri was organist there so it wasn't trespassing. Anyway, a village church in Wales is open and accessible for worship twenty-four hours a day. No one would ever think of desecrating it. I showed her the organ where Ceri sat to play the hymns. She was attentive to everything and was wonderfully well-behaved on these outings, though the walking was often too much for her short puppy-legs. So we didn't go too far from home and rested often. We were getting along famously and learning, little by little, about each other every day.

Afternoons she liked best, when we went for a bus ride to Llandysul, the next town. Dogs, if accompanied by adults, are allowed on buses, and everywhere else in Wales—that's if they are well-behaved and she was. Coming home from Llandysul, she was all tuckered out with the sights and sounds of town life and slept quietly in my lap. She revelled in the attention the townsfolk gave her, for she was an extremely friendly little puppy and we got many a smile on the main street, and later, waiting for the bus to go home.

Llandysul is a busy, thriving Cardiganshire town, noted for its woolen mills principally, and Ceridwen loved its hustle and bustle. In fact I discovered immediately she liked people better than Glindy did, his affection being reserved chiefly for his mistress and the people who had a relationship with *her*.

Once we took a long ride to New Castle Emlyn, some six miles away, near Brongest, the village where my father was born. But our visiting day happened to be a Wednesday, when all the New Castle Emlyn shops were closed, and Ceridwen didn't like the deserted streets. She missed the excitement and attention at Llandysul, but accepted the disappointment resignedly. All the way home she sat blissfully happy in my lap, occasionally raising her head to peep out the bus window. What a good-natured little puppy she was, I noted with satisfaction.

All during the fortnight's stay I was preparing her for the day she would be leaving Cross Hill Farm forever, remembering how lonely Glindy had been after he left it to fly to America. At the same time, I was readying her precious mother, Linda Lassie, for our departure, knowing what a loss we would be to her, one of the sweetest corgis that ever lived. I dreaded the heartbreak that was inevitably drawing near. Linda Lassie felt it too, for everytime we went to Llandysul she came to the gate with us and looked longingly after us, then waited patiently at the gate until we returned home.

Thus we dreaded the day we would be leaving Cross Hill Farm forever, and almost wished it would never come. But come it did, and I will never forget Linda Lassie's pleading eyes the day we left the Farm for good. She clung to Ceridwen and me, unwilling to let us go, begging to come with us, while her little daughter was happy as a lark, unaware she would never see her mother again. Ceri and Rose finally had to put Linda Lassie in the barn, so she wouldn't see us actually leaving.

* * * * *

There were no problems on the plane trip to America. Ceri drove Ceridwen and me to the railroad station in Carmarthen for the long train journey to Cardiff, where we connected with the bus for the airport and the plane trip to New York. She behaved beautifully on the train, sitting quietly in my lap or on the seat beside me all the way to Cardiff; but wasn't permitted to sit with me on the plane. I worried about how she would fare in the plane's baggage room until I learned it was uncrowded, was pressurized and the baggage master had placed her crate comfortably away from draughts and excessive vibration. I stayed with her until take-off time and that was all I was allowed to do by the airport personnel.

She went through Customs and Health requirements in New York like a breeze, but the airport itself was a madhouse, the lengthy 1966 airways strike still being in force, as it had been when I went over *to* Wales to get her. We won't go here into the ordeal it was to carry the little four-months-old puppy, who like Glindy couldn't walk on the slippery air terminal floors, while kicking my two large suitcases, no porter to be had for love or money in such a madhouse.

We were rescued finally by a little Irish Airways lass, who had been watching us from her desk, and couldn't stand the sight any longer, even though it wasn't her problem. She proved an angel in disguise and expertly got us to our Pittsburgh plane by the skin of our teeth just as it was taking off. There were strike complications at Greater Pittsburgh Airport Terminal also, but those we didn't mind because we were almost home.

* * * * *

Chapter 2

THERE WAS CERIDWEN

The Confrontation

Glindy was away at a very good boarding kennel, several miles from Pittsburgh, while I was in Wales getting Ceridwen and he wasn't to be picked up until the day after my homecoming. My brother had promised to drive Ceridwen and me to the kennel to get him as it had been prearranged with the kennel people that we would drop her off at their first gate, a quarter of a mile down the road from the main driveway and entrance. They were to keep her for two hours or thereabouts while my brother and I drove away, the assumption being that this would give the two dogs a chance to get well-acquainted, so that by the time we got back to pick them up, they would be lifelong friends; and there would be no problems.

But things didn't work out that way. For, just as we entered their main driveway on the way back, through the window in the back seat of the car, I saw Glindy suddenly stiffening and looking wildly in the direction of our car. He evidently had gotten my scent and was almost crazy with excitement. So the kennel people had to separate him and Ceridwen and hurry her out of sight into another kennel area while I jumped out of the car to greet my beloved Glindy, now mutely overcome with emotion at seeing me. I walked him up and down the kennel yard saying soothing things, telling him how much I had missed him, how wonderful he looked—which was true, for the kennel people had taken excellent care of him and he was absolutely handsome. All the while I was talking to him my heart was pounding, his was too, almost to the breaking point.

When our reunion was over Ceridwen was brought out of hiding and she greeted me as though I belonged to *her*, but Glindy would have none of that and expertly dominated the scene. It was a heartbreaking dilemma for the three of us, and we had an awful time on the ride back to Pittsburgh. The dogs and I sat in the back seat, one on each side of me, both growling audibly and claiming my attention, each rightfully deeming me his own. It was pure anguish for all of us, my brother included, and the whole ride home was a nightmare.

The month that followed was the same, with Glindy and Ceridwen wrangling and fighting with each other every day. I spent hours trying to pacify them, explaining that this was ''home'' for all of us now, all the while blaming myself for the dilemma. What was happening was certainly not Ceridwen's fault, for she had done no wrong. Nor was it Glindy's fault that he couldn't divine my motive for bringing her into our home and looked upon it as rank treachery.

I prayed and worked at peacemaking every day for almost five weeks until at last, all at once, came the day we were out of our dilemma. It sounds trite to say that love found the way, but this was true. Love and the sterling qualities of both dogs. Strangely, Ceridwen settled things by loving Glindy more than anything or anyone else in the world, including me; and Glindy settled things by finally conquering his jealousy, and accepting her as a member of our family at first, and later as his loving mate and companion.

There never had been any doubt in my mind, then or at any time, who was uppermost in my heart, or that Glindy's place could ever be usurped by another dog, even little Ceridwen. But stupidly, and because I was as involved in the matter as they were, I hadn't realized that his love for me would be so great as to temporarily derange him. Ceridwen's insight *did* see this, however, and with her healing love, she made him well again. Dogs are nobler than people in situations like this—at least Glindy and Ceridwen were. The submissive role for her; the protective, aggressive role for him, ever after worked beautifully. Besides there was something masterful, a certain air of distinction about Glindy, that Ceridwen and I both recognized and deferred to. In other words, he was "boss" to both of us.

* * * * *

Ceridwen, did you do that?

This is not to say that little Miss Ceridwen suddenly achieved sainthood, and that Glindy took on the wings of an angel, and all our days were serene ever after. Far from it. She was experiencing the normal growing pains of a healthy puppy that first year of her life and was diabolically given to puppy mischief, busy every minute of the day scouting and scooting around the apartment for things to tear apart: electric wiring, rugs, blanket-bindings, bathroom fixtures, rubber mats, anything, everything chewable. She carried things from room to room, then set them down all around her, proud of her collection. She chewed through pillows, tossing their insides about like snowflakes in a TV snowstorm.

We lived in a world of shredded newspapers and sloshed through mountains of them daily. Objects unseen and forgotten for years met us everywhere as her merry little backside shook with determination dragging them out of cupboard hideaways. Looking at me innocently while she was busy at her mischief, I often didn't realize she had done something until the mischief was already done. "Ceridwen was here" might well have been written on every bedpost, wall and floor in our apartment that first year of her life as rivers of toilet paper and balls of fluff greeted us everywhere until Glindy and I blinked our eyes at the sight of them.

In one week she ripped off the valance of my favorite chair, divested a hassock of its sawdust entrails, then sat down in the middle of the mess feasting on the sawdust; she chewed an oval rug to shreds, and a rubber mat to confetti. Some wainscoting and flooring in the hallway only escaped mutilation because she was too tuckered out by the time she got to them.

Glindy's yard, too, was a shambles. She dug holes assiduously in it and took her rest in the petunia bed, or alongside the geraniums, snipping off buds as the spirit moved her. Glindy watched it all with interest, obviously having the time of his life, for he had never even *dreamed* of such mayhem, but from the look on his face was evidently wishing he had.

Feeding her too was an everlasting problem. What to give a puppy with a bottomless tummy, when we had been accustomed to Glindy, a finicky eater at best, presented a daily puzzle. And no matter *what* she was eating, delicious or otherwise, part of her attention was devoted to removing bobby pins from my hair, as I stooped to adjust her dish, or to pick up food particles she hadn't gobbled down.

* * * * *

Love Aborning . . .

Yet for all her teasing and tomboyish ways, she was definitely feminine. This was interesting to watch after being exposed to Glindy's masculinity for six years. She loved to be fussed over and would perk herself up self-consciously when told she looked pretty; and she was the cuddliest little lump of canine flesh God ever put breath into. Curling herself up into a ball like a kitten, she sank contentedly into my lap, or anywhere she took a fancy to, and went to sleep.

From the start she was a bigger and heavier-boned corgi than Glindy, more flashy too in her coat and markings. Even in her roguish ways there was an air of pride, a dignity about her. Scoldings brought Glindy to his knees, figuratively speaking. Ceridwen accepted them with disdain, though once I did find her hiding disconsolately under my bed, after a scolding. No one could budge her into anything unless she felt so inclined. I had learned that way back in Cross Hill Farm days, at our first meeting.

Life those days was hectic, yet it was good for all three of us and we were wonderfully busy and happy. Glindy was eating better than he ever had and he was much more frisky. He was becoming less set in his ways, too, and less like an only child in a family. Evidently some of Ceridwen's philosophical disposition was rubbing off on him. When he stretched out on the floor she flopped down too, right beside him; when he nibbled grass, so did she; if he changed his position in the yard, which he did a dozen times a day, she invariably gave up her cozy nook, and trotted devotedly after him, to some lesser lair.

While they were alike as two peas in a pod in some ways, in other ways they were quite different. She was more supple than Glindy had ever been, and was lithe and lissome as an eel when she didn't want to be picked up, slithering away from your grasp. She became a shameless coquette with Glindy, bumping into him, throwing herself at him wantonly Mae West-fashion, using every wile at her command, to get his attention. This accomplished, there was a fearful tussle, with who's ahead? your guess as good as mine. In cold weather her nose became red, like Rudolph the red-nosed reindeer, though she wasn't snow-crazy like Rudy, nor even like Glindy, who in his early days had been a Veritable Snowman. A mouthful of "the white stuff" was enough for Miss Ceridwen.

Another difference was Glindy didn't like to be laughed at, but the louder you laughed at Ceridwen, the better she liked it, and she usually joined in the merriment with a grin that at times was bewitched. Her determination was monumental, and a sudden noise could send her into a panic. There was the time she and I were walking in Edgewood Park. An automobile exhaust backfired with a loud bang. Ceridwen broke away from me with the strength of a lion, her leash trailing, and took off like lightning.

Traffic both directions came to a dead halt as her determined little body propelled her on. I yelled to a boy across the street "catch her and I'll give you a quarter." He took off, but was no match for Miss Ceridwen. Then I stopped worrying, for suddenly it was plain to be seen she was headed for home and knew *exactly* where she was going. Nothing, no one stopped her either, until she reached our front porch, where she was sitting when I finally got there, the boy having given up the chase along the way.

In the first year of her life, Ceridwen's friendliness and good-will were a delight to see. She simply loved everything and everybody. She even loved bugs. Ants and bees were her specialties, yet they never stung or bit her as they did Glindy. Nudging insects at their work was her favorite outdoor sport, and she watched ants working for hours, while lying on her tummy in the yard. She hadn't an enemy of her own in the world during those months though she did take on Glindy's enemies. For example, the two of them carried on a running feud with the next-door milkman, because he once told Glindy to "shut up!"

All this while she was becoming an excellent companion for Glindy, and an ideal mate, which augured well for the day we would ultimately mate them and have puppies to carry on their lines.

Chapter 3

HER PEDIGREE AND FAMILY TREE

CERIDWEN ROSE – A PEDIGREE

(Born April 18, 1966, at Cross Hill Farm,
Llanfihangel Ar Arth, Carmarthenshire)

The Kennel Club (London) Export Registration Certificate 87860/66.
American Kennel Club Registration Certificate WA 792309.

Parents	Grandparents	Great-Grandparents
SIRE	3. Falaise Tom Tit of St. Mabyn	7. Ch. Maracas Masterpiece
		8. St. Mabyn's Golden Shandie
1. Stormerbanks Tom Cobley	4. Ch. Stormerbanks Superfine	9. Stormerbanks Supersonic
		10. Tresarden Trinket
	5. Larkwhistle Lucifer	11. Stormerbanks Ambrose
DAM		12. Ch. Larkwhistle Lucinda of Almadee
2. Linda Lassie	6. Cleddau Clover	13. Crymmch Challenge
		14. Heatherrose Dusty

An Appraisal

Ceridwen never had much use for her "family tree," literally or figuratively, but since she was at all times a potential show dog, having the necessary qualifications for such a career, and dog people like to follow such things, let's stop for a minute to discuss her pedigree.

You have already learned she was destined to be a loving wife and mother, and was chosen for that role by her mistress. This mission she fulfilled admirably – no one could have done better. Therefore in *that,* she was a "champion" of the highest order – as high as any dog in the show-ring.

An appraisal of her pedigree brings to light these interesting facts; and you can evaluate them for yourself, if you're a follower and admirer of the corgi breed.

She had three champions in her immediate "family tree": Champion Stormerbanks Superfine, Champion Maracas Masterpiece, and Champion Larkwhistle Lucinda of Almadee, all of them long-standing celebrities in the Corgi Halls of Fame in Great Britain and throughout the world, even before she was born.

Her grandmother *Champion Stormerbanks Superfine* was as lovely a corgi as ever saw the light of day. Born in 1955, a champion the year after, her beautiful face, figure and bearing won her fame at British dog shows during her lifetime; and it is from "Superfine" Ceridwen has inherited her expressive face and lovely markings.

Great-Grandfather *Maracas Masterpiece* was famous in British dog circles before I ever heard of a corgi, or knew what the breed looked like. Born in 1952, he sired numerous sons and daughters who became champions on both sides of the Atlantic, and whose descendants still flourish in the corgi world.

Larkwhistle Lucinda of Almadee, her great-grandmother, the third Champion in the Ceridwen family tree, won five Challenge Certificates in her day. While, she, Superfine and Maracas light up the family tree bountifully, there are other luminaries among the branches, such as Crymmch Challenge, Tresarden Trinket, Falaise Tom Tit of St. Mabyn, Stormerbanks Supersonic, and so on, that have kept the light still shining.

Ceridwen's "mom" and "dad" were admirable corgis too. *Linda Lassie,* her mother, I have already mentioned as being the best-natured corgi ever born. Her father *Stormerbanks Tom Cobley* (or "Cobbleigh," as it is sometimes spelled) deserves mention too, being of an entirely different temperament. A fun-loving, man-about-town sort of fellow, he had been aptly named by his breeder, Pat Hewan of British corgi fame, after a character of the same name in an old English ballard "Widdecombe Fair." The original "Old Uncle Tom Cobley" was evidently quite a gay blade in his day and amusingly, Ceridwen's father, his namesake, was a good bit like him. So we can presume some of her teasing ways have been inherited from her father.

You might be interested in the "Widdecombe Fair" ballad in its entirety, because it's a well-known favorite among balladeers even today, Burl Ives among them. So we're giving it to you on this page, and you can see that a balladeer has plenty to work with in this quaint tale about a mare and his carefree friends at the "Fair," in the Merry Old England of long ago.

Copied from the *Oxford Book of Ballads* by Arthur Quiller Couch.

WIDDECOMBE FAIR

1.

Tom Pearse, Tom Pearse, lend me your grey mare
　　All along, down along, out along, lee
For I want for to go to Widdecombe Fair
　　Wi' Bill Brewer, Jan Stewer, Peter Gurney, Peter Davy,
　　　Dan'l Whiddon, Harry Hawk
Old Uncle Tom Cobbleigh and all.
　　　Chorus: Old Uncle Tom Cobbleigh and all.

2.

And when shall I see again my grey mare?
　　All along, down along, out along, lee.
By Friday soon, or Saturday noon,
　　Wi' Bill Brewer, Jan Stewer, Peter Gurney, Peter Davy,
　　　Dan'l Whiddon, Harry Hawk,
Old Uncle Tom Cobbleigh and all.
　　　Chorus: Old Uncle Tom Cobbleigh and all.

3.

Then Friday came, and Saturday noon,
　　All along, down along, out along, lee.
But Tom Pearse's old mare hath not trotted home,
　　With Bill Brewer, Jan Stewer, Peter Gurney, Peter Davy,
　　　Dan'l Whiddon, Harry Hawk,
Old Uncle Tom Cobbleigh and all.
　　　Chorus: Old Uncle Tom Cobbleigh and all.

4.

So Tom Pearse he got up to the top o' the hill,
　　All along, down along, out along, lee.
And he seed his old mare down a-making her will
　　With Bill Brewer, Jan Stewer, Peter Gurney, Peter Davy,
　　　Dan'l Whiddon, Harry Hawk,
Old Uncle Tom Cobbleigh and all.
　　　Chorus: Old Uncle Tom Cobbleigh and all.

5.

So Tom Pearse's old mare, her took sick and her died,
    All along, down along, out along, lee.
And Tom he sat down on a stone, and he cried
    With Bill Brewer, Jan Stewer, Peter Gurney, Peter Davy,
        Dan'l Whiddon, Harry Hawk,
Old Uncle Tom Cobbleigh and all.
        Chorus: Old Uncle Tom Cobbleigh and all.

6.

But this isn't the end o' this shocking affair,
    All along, down along, out along, lee.
Nor, though *they* be dead, of the horrid career
    of Bill Brewer, Jan Stewer, Peter Gurney, Peter Davy,
        Dan'l Whiddon, Harry Hawk,
Old Uncle Tom Cobbleigh and all.
        Chorus: Old Uncle Tom Cobbleigh and all.

7.

When the wind whistles cold on the moor of a night,
    All along, down along, out along, lee
Tom Pearse's old mare doth appear, ghostly white,
    With Bill Brewer, Jan Stewer, Peter Gurney, Peter Davy,
        Dan'l Whiddon, Harry Hawk
Old Uncle Tom Cobbleigh and all.
    Chorus: Old Uncle Tom Cobbleigh and all.

8.

And all the long night he heard skirling and groans,
    All along, down along, out along, lee.
From Tom Pearse's old mare in her rattling bones,
    And from Bill Brewer, Jan Stewer, Peter Gurney, Peter Davy,
        Dan'l Whiddon, Harry Hawk
Old Uncle Tom Cobbleigh and all.
    Chorus: Old Uncle Tom Cobbleigh and all.

Well, there you are, if you're still with us, for you might conceivably have wandered off, feeling ballads and the like a far cry from the Ceridwen family tree. If so, we apologize for this injected bit of humor about her father's name. What's in a name, you are asking? Well this one at least has something in it and the Tom Cobley touch might very well account, as we've already said, for some of the Ceridwen caprices.

Chapter 4

LIFE WITH GLINDY

Up to now, Life With Glindy, for the little heroine of our story had been concerned with her growing-up days and activities. Here, we will have a look at her as a more mature being, with characteristics well-formed, and a wisdom and philosophical nature all her own. Temperamentally a more adaptable creature than Glindy — after she gave herself over to love for him in the early days, it was a permanent, unchangeable relationship. Everything related to him, and this was an expedient, compatible arrangement for both of them; and worked well in the day-to-day pattern of life for all three of us.

There were ups and downs of course but they were minor, and the endless attempts at mating them, while hectic, had lent to turbulent living at times, no doubt about it. Ceridwen was the sexiest of sirens at such times, and this was a surprise, when measured against her usual serenity. She just wouldn't let him alone during her "seasons," and spent most of her time trying to entice him, which naturally, he liked, but being a male he was sometimes more aggressive in his responses than Cerid could handle. So there were many moving and maniacal moments as they chased each other around, in our otherwise sedate house.

Don't let anyone ever tell you that Nature knows best about such matters. Nature knew nothing about how to handle Glindy's and Cerid's lovemaking and was just as dumb as the rest of us about keeping things under control. We never could have managed the mating of them without *professional* help, and they never would have produced offspring if left to their own clumsy devices. For one of Cerid's "seasons" we were offered help, and invited to a friend's home in California, for a month. She was a well-known, successful breeder of poodles on the West Coast, but she met her Waterloo with Glindy and Cerid. Corgis are difficult to breed, at least Glindy and Cerid were, and the California climate, so widely touted for its salutary benefits, didn't do anything for our twosome.

But enough of this sort of talk before you get to thinking that's all there was to "Life With Glindy." Not so. "Seasons" may come and seasons may go, but walking goes on forever, and our Glindy was an inveterate walker. Cerid, therefore, in time reluctantly became one. Walking two dogs on city streets is sometimes a formidable task, however, and has its hazards when encountering other dogs on the loose, so we had some exciting moments. Ceridwen let Glindy handle the encounters, but since he was willing to take on any adversary, regardless of size, the burden of the encounters usually fell on their mistress. Naturally there were lively skirmishes.

Speaking of Cerid's "seasons" again, they were a nuisance in more ways than one. One nuisance, and a trying one, was that every time she came into season, except the two times she actually *did* conceive and have puppies, we went through what were called "false pregnancies," those inexplicable visitations of Mother Nature that put a female dog through the whole birthing cycle right up to the delivery date, all for nothing, and without anything to show for her ordeal but a mysteriously diminished abdomen at the end of it all, just as though there had been a *real* pregnancy and litter.

Glindy was as involved in these false pregnancies as Cerid was, since he always lost his little walking-companion and playmate for their duration, because of her increased size and difficulty with walking at such times. We remember a humorous incident with a *real* pregnancy and Cerid's first litter. The veterinarian had told us to take her temperature periodically for the last couple of days before delivery time, because this would foretell the imminence of the prospective puppies. Much to our astonishment, Glindy wanted *his* temperature taken, too, and really became huffed if we didn't take it.

There was a humorous time too, with Ceridwen's *second* litter. The vet had told us to bellyband Ceridwen's midriff *after the delivery* of the puppies, so her bodily shape would return to normal, since so many female dogs (women too) lose their shapes after having babies. Glindy wanted *his* midriff "bellybanded" too, and gave me no peace until I pinned a wide band around his tummy. He was as proud as could be of that bellyband, and the neighbors had a good "belly laugh," when they saw him in the yard wearing it.

However, there was a sadness connected with Cerid's first litter, in which Glindy became *so* involved he nearly died. Temporarily Cerid was so deeply immersed in her mothering she forgot about the idol of her life and gave him no attention whatsoever. He went into such a state of grief and shock, his body developed a tumor, and he became paralyzed and couldn't walk. We made several trips to a nearby vet with him because our vet was on an extended holiday trip. The nearby vet suggested putting him to sleep but I wouldn't think of it.

It was a terrible catastrophe for all of us because Glindy doubted *my* love, too, and believed when I had to spend so much time with Ceridwen and her babies, that *I* didn't love *him* any more, which was unthinkable. At times you could actually hear him crying, but he wouldn't come near me or let me go near him, even though I was pouring out my very soul with love towards him. Cerid was busy raising her little ruffians and she never realized the great harm she was doing him. That was *my* burden and entailed weeks of patient, prayerful understanding and love while working with his sick body and mind. He didn't get better and walk again properly until the puppies were all sold, and went to new homes.

Actually, Glindy never took much interest in Cerid's puppies, even when they were his own offspring, and it is doubtful he would ever have been a doting father. He just wasn't the type, but his capacity for deep affection was unassailable, as exemplified *first* in his attachment to me — "love at first sight" you could call it; and *second* in his increasing affection for Cerid as the years went on. Thus her indifference at puppy time wounded him almost irreparably while it lasted.

Yet "Life With Glindy" with all its ups and downs, was full of diversion for them *and* for me. There were the times they stayed with Stephanie Heitzman at her boarding kennel — and liked it — when I was vacationing. There were also brief stays for one or both of them that came with trips to the vet's hospital for inoculations, minor ailments and so on, and there were plenty of other distractions and diversions for all of us.

For despite his sobriety Glindy could be highly entertaining and a real clown at times and he never failed to amuse and entertain Ceridwen and me. When we had visitors, for instance, he "sang" for our guests (at least we called it singing), just like the dog in the TV commercial that sings for his supper in the dog-food ad. Cerid and I, as well as our visitors, liked to hear him sing; he was such an obliging performer and so comical, we applauded him enthusiastically after *every* performance. Cerid was in her seventh heaven at such times — pleased and proud that *her* Glindy was the center of attention.

In fact, summing it all up: "Life With Ceridwen for *Glindy*" was life replete and "Life With Glindy" for *Ceridwen* was everything!

Growing-up and relaxing in our Farm House on the Hill, with Glindy (her beloved) pictured on the lower-left bottom row of pictures.

Chapter 5

MOTHERHOOD – THE BEST AND THE WORST OF IT

Glindy was a healthy, handsome male corgi and had all the potential for being a good stud dog, even though he was inexperienced. Ceridwen was a healthy, handsome female corgi, and had every potential for motherhood, but she too was inexperienced; and corgis have always been known to be difficult to breed.

So it was a long time, and after many a try, that she at length became a mother; and then at first it wasn't a mother to Glindy's offspring as we had long hoped and prayed, but to Champion Ehrstag's Farleu, a fine-looking male corgi living not far from our Banksville home. Farleu was owned by Mr. Clark Frame and had gone "Best of Breed" at the Sewickley Dog Show only the Saturday before he was bred to Ceridwen. We hadn't known this when we summoned the courage to ask Mr. Frame if he would consider breeding Farleu to Ceridwen, but being a true-blue corgi lover, he understood our breeding problem and obligingly consented to the mating. He asked only that he might have the pick of the litter in lieu of a stud fee, and that his vet, and no other, should attend the breeding and birthing. We were on our way, and off to a good start.

We won't here go into the details of the breeding, gestation-period and actual birthing of the fine litter of seven puppies that resulted. Suffice to say, all went well and the Frames were well-pleased. So was Ceridwen's mistress for both Farleu and Ceridwen had distinguished themselves. With the experience of a litter behind her and proof that there was nothing wrong with Cerid's ability to produce one, we could once more be hopeful for a Glindy litter, our ultimate goal, next time round when she came into season.

She was an excellent mother, our little Ceridwen, giving her all to hers and Farleu's babes. It's a wonder any canine mother can have much love for her little ones when, according to custom, they are taken away from her a month or so after weaning-time to be sold, and she has gone through the whole ordeal of carrying her babes, birthing them, and raising them, with nothing to show for her trouble but a feeling of loss.

But love her little ones, Ceridwen did, and she enjoyed the mothering too, while they were with her, but when they left for their new homes she went back to Glindy, the *real* love of her life, whom she had forsaken during the mothering period. He, shocked at her seeming perfidy, had suffered great grief during that period as we have already told you. But though he didn't realize it at the time, she was only obeying the law of Nature in her mothering experience and *not* actually casting him aside, such a thought being unthinkable to her.

Going back to that first mothering experience, it was something to see our fun-loving little philosopher turn to the exhausting duties of motherhood with all her heart and physical resources. Farleu had been an excellent sire with his even-tempered disposition matching hers, and it was quite a feather in Ceridwen's cap to have had a litter to him. We could reasonably expect good-tempered, well-balanced puppies from their union. Three of those puppies are still thriving today as this is being written, more than eleven years later. You'll be hearing more about these three in a later chapter.

Those were the happy days, the days of that first litter. Ceridwen romped and played unrestrainedly with her babes. Ruffians they were, too, thumping and jumping all over their poor mother until her bones must have ached with their enthusiasm.

Little *Sweetie Pie* and *Foxie* died at two months of age, but might have been living today too, if their inexperienced mistress had only known about the gas in their tummies and how to expel it. Four, however, *did* reach selling age when they were three months old, the first to be sold being the one we playfully called *Jumbo* because he was the biggest of the clan. He was his mother's favorite, too, and went to a Welsh couple in Minnesota. The one we nicknamed "Mickey Mouse," because she darted about like her famous namesake, went to Mr. Frame, as his pick of the litter. The one called *"Precious"* (because she really was) went to a young lawyer and his family in Atlanta, Georgia; and the one we called *"Honey"* (because she looked like a streak of it with her coat of burnished gold) went to a Welsh-born couple in Kinston, North Carolina. All of their nicknames had to be dropped, of course, when they were registered with American Kennel Club and received their pedigreed names.

Little "Honey" was with us for a fortnight longer than the others, while waiting for the go-sign to send her to her new home. In those two weeks she really became a little "honey" to all of us, including Glindy, who had not at any time been chummy with the others. With her departure, the saga of Cerid's first litter was ended, and our household went back to its normal routine. Now we could hope once again for a successful mating with Glindy.

* * * * *

Our Goal Is Achieved At Last!

Frankly we had just about given up on this hope. There had been so many false pregnancies, so many heartaches and disappointments with breeding attempts, we saw little reason to disrupt our present serenity and harmony to worry again about mating the two of them. For it had begun to strike me this was only my *own* selfish idea—they themselves being supremely happy without offspring. That was the state of affairs the day of the Western Pennsylvania Kennel Association 1970 Annual Dog Show at the Civic Arena, when I went there.

But "God works in a mysterious way, His wonders to perform" and almost the first person I saw at the show was our old friend Stephanie Heitzman, an active exhibitor and participant at *all* local dog shows, and a loyal friend of Glindy and Cerid, who in times past had made various attempts to mate them. Cerid just happened to be in season for the umpteenth time and when Stevie learned this, she jolted me out of my complacency by asking: "Are you going to try to mate the two of them again?"

"No," I told her, "you of *all* people should know we have already tried hard enough. So we'll just pass it up this time around."

"Aw, come now, don't be a quitter," Stevie retorted. "Try it once more and I'll help you." There we were again into "the mating game," without my slightest inclination. But, because Stevie had helped with so many breeding attempts and was such an excellent breeder and loyal friend, I said yes to her. She came the following week for Glindy and Cerid, to keep them for a few days at her kennel "to see what happens," said she, generously.

Well, the rest is history, but I say truthfully and am sure Stevie will agree, this was about all the thought either of us gave to the matter during the next several weeks. But gradually, as the weeks wore on, it struck me I ought, for safety's sake, to take Cerid to the vet for an examination "just in case." Stevie was by then out ot of town a lot and I hadn't heard from her, but more than owed it to her to follow through.

The vet said it was too late to fully examine Cerid for fear of hurting any puppies there *might* be, but told me to bring her back to his hospital two or three days before the expiration of the normal gestation period, and he would take care of the birthing again, should there be one, and that was that.

To this day, I can't get over the wonder of it all, and the miracle of Cerid's second litter. Here was the fulfillment of my fondest dream: a litter from Glindy. It had come so quietly I couldn't comprehend it and felt dumb with disbelief when I saw the eight squirming puppies—Glindy's and Cerid's offspring—right before my eyes. Truly it was a miracle—their Creator's miracle—and Stevie and I could hardly take credit for it, we being no more than the instruments of God's plan.

Cerid was in labor fifteen hours this second time. Neither of her two birthings had been easy but the first one had been infinitely easier than the second one. Motherhood, for her, the second time was also a more serious affair than the first time, for her body had been severely wracked by the long, drawn-out birthing. After it was over, she withdrew deeply into herself and family, rejecting Glindy *again* as she had with her first litter, but even more visibly and forcibly. Glindy, the idol of her life! And he too was more fiercely resentful of her indifference. Therefore, for safety's sake, he couldn't be included in her family circle at all those first months of his fatherhood.

We've already said there were eight, but only six grew to adulthood, one having died the day it was born, already half-dead when it emerged from its mother's womb. The second fatality was little Cariad (Welsh for love), who put up a colossal fight for his life, but finally succumbed after seventeen days on earth. They all had Welsh names, prefixed by "Glyncerid," the combination of Glindy's and Cerid's names.

At first the puppies were too small for "Papa" to notice. Added to this, Cerid was too possessive a mother to allow the intrusion even of their father into the family circle. I tried not to worry about it though Glindy was a problem, and I *did* scold Cerid from time to time for her treatment of the lonely little "head of the family." But in all fairness to her, the puppies took so much of her time (mine too) it was all she could do to rear them. Later, they got to be such rowdies they were often too much for her and had to be watched constantly for fear of getting into hurtful mischief and unduly annoying their father. They were all beautiful, healthy babies, a credit to both of their parents.

Cerid seemed not to have any favorites in this second litter and they all shared equally in her love and attention. But as already mentioned, the sad thing about a canine mother is she doesn't get enough time to enjoy her babes, the way a human mother does, since they are all sold so early in life and she never sees them after they're sold. Though she *is* spared the sorrows of a human mother whose children sometimes grow up to be heartaches. Lucky she was, too, that she couldn't follow through on what happened to her babes in the second litter, for all but one of them (the one exception being Twm Shon Catti) had untimely ends, and went to Heaven before they were five years old. Read their heartrending stories in the following paragraphs.

Allie, an abbreviation for "Allelulia," was the little charmer that went farthest away, to his new home in San Francisco. Strangely, too, he was the first to die, at approximately three and a half years of age, and I use the word "strangely" because it was such a quick and mysterious death even the veterinarian was unsure of its cause. He finally attributed it to a kidney infection thought to have been contracted from errant squirrels in the park where Allie went for his daily walks, squirrels being known carriers of deadly diseases. His Welsh San Francisco mistress and her family were devastated by his untimely loss.

Teivi Tim and *Angharad* both had shocking deaths when they were about four and a half years old — too shocking to dwell upon. Teivi Tim had been bought by a doctor and his family in northern Ohio. Where they lived there was a next-door neighbor who was mentally ill, but would not seek psychiatric help. One day when Teivi was sitting in his own backyard (which he loved to do), the man next door went completely berserk and ran out of the house with a shotgun, bent on shooting his wife. Seeing little Teivi Tim first, he inexplicably pointed the gun at Teivi and killed him outright.

Somehow this broke the tension in the man's confused brain, and brought on violent sobs, for he loved Teivi dearly. It also led to his seeking psychiatric attention, and in due course he was cured. When Teivi Tim's family finally wrote to tell me about the tragedy, I could read between the lines that they were consoling themselves as well as me, by saying he had not died in vain, and was actually a martyr, having averted a murder. Maybe so, but this was poor comfort to me.

Angharad, the little beauty of Glindy's and Cerid's litter, had just as tragic an end. She had been re-sold by her first owner to the young niece of a dog show judge, who had long admired her. The niece was planning to breed her, and was the owner of a small kennel of nine champion corgis somewhere in Ohio. Ohio, as you may know, sometimes suffers destructive tornadoes and hurricanes, and other such natural disasters. There came one that made headlines all over the USA. It struck the niece's kennel by lightning, and all the lovely champions — every one of them, and Angharad also, died of asphyxiation before they could be rescued. The young owner of the kennel went into such a state of shock she never again returned to the world of dogs. The tragedy had proved too much for her.

This leaves *Myfanwy, Twm Shon Catti* and *Bensalem,* the other three members of Glindy's and Cerid's family.

Myfanwy (we called her "Muv" to rhyme with Love) was the one that most resembled Glindy and was bought by a Pittsburgh organist and his family, all of whom adored her. One morning she was playing outdoors as usual, shortly after the two children of the household had gone to school, when she was seized by violent pains. Her distracted mistress rushed her to the veterinarian, who diagnosed it as a kidney seizure and asked to keep her overnight in his hospital for observation. But before the children got home from school, that very day, he had phoned to say that Muv had suddenly died. The family never got over her loss and even to this day when I see them at musicals around Pittsburgh, they can't speak of Muv without tears in their eyes.

Bensalem (Benjie) the firstborn of the litter and the largest, lived happily in his Beaver Valley Home, not far from Pittsburgh, for nearly five years until one day, out of a clear blue sky, an out-of-state automobile drove up to his house when the little boy of the family was at school, and his mother was at the supermarket. Before anyone realized what was happening Benjie was spirited away in the speeding automobile. The dog-napping was done so quickly that the neighbors were unsure it was a theft until the car started to pick up speed before it vanished. Though the abduction was widely advertised, with a generous reward for Benjie's return, he was never seen again. We can only hope his captor, who must have known something about the handsome little corgi, has been kind to him, and that he is still alive today.

Which brings us to *Twm Shon Catti* (Twm). Twm — the sole remaining reminder of that beautiful, much loved, much-prayed-for litter of Glindy and Cerid still thrives, and lives in the hearts of his owners today at well over nine years of age, in a suburb of Pittsburgh. He is the apple-of-their-eye and no one could be happier than he with them, and they with him, a mutual happiness which has grown through the years.

There is a picture of Twm in chapter twelve. We will have more to say about him and his owners, Mr. and Mrs. John C. Istvan, in that chapter.

Glindy's and Cerid's sextet at nine weeks: (left to right) Angharad, Twm Shon Catti, Allelulia, Bensalem, Myfanwy and Teivy Tim.

Chapter 6

WE MOVE FROM OUR HOUSE ON THE HILL
AND GLINDY GOES TO HEAVEN

The three of us had lived happily and well for almost six years in "the house of the hill," as my friends called our little abode atop *such* a high terrace there were thirty-one steps to our front door. However, this didn't bother us much because we hardly ever used the front door, having no need to with all the other entrances available.

Our home and "castle" was on an embankment with a cement walk-around, and a quarter of an acre of property surrounded by a fence, and there was even a patio if we wanted to use it. The front porch, where we did most of our living during the summer, was attached to the front of the house and was surrounded by a closed-in railing adorned with a sturdy, always-locked gate, thus making it a safe and private haven for all of us. The former owners had loved the house and added all sorts of accommodations through the years, the husband being handy at carpentering and such manly arts.

Thus the porch was a godsend for Glindy, and later for the puppies, both litters having used it to their heart's content. We used to say jokingly, if a burglar ever felt rash enough to ascend all the steps to the front door to rob us, we'd give him a cup of tea and a cushion to rest on, before chasing him off the premises.

Glindy and Cerid had the whole world to look out upon and bark at in our pseudo-mountain retreat, and it was a ready-made heaven. But dogs and men (women, too) *do* grow old and they do have to eat. Our supermarket was three blocks away and, without a car or a helicopter, this was a problem. Both dogs loved their daily walk, too, in the world below with its attractions. So there came a day when they and their mistress found the going a bit rough for their short legs and her short wind.

So after the second litter came and went we decided there were to be no more litters. With no more necessity for such a lofty abode, we reluctantly resolved to move to some easier place to live in. Glindy was more than thirteen years old, Ceridwen more than seven. They, like their mistress, were feeling their ages. Thus we moved to the newly-built, high-rise Senior Citizens' apartment building in the Lawrenceville area of Pittsburgh — which had ample grounds for Glindy and Cerid to roam around in, and other accommodations — expecting to live comfortably for the rest of our lives.

But sorrow came to us soon. Glindy lived only another seven months, when a hidden cancer cruelly took his life. Nothing was the same thereafter for Ceridwen and me. It was a cruel, fateful blow; never again were we a happy "family." We were now just another lonely twosome, with our idol and head of the house gone.

The next several months saw a new and different Ceridwen emerging, perceptively changed in her ways and habits. But first before telling you about that, we'll tell you about the "Sanctuary." There wasn't the peace and privacy of our "house-on-the-hill," in our new apartment-home, but at least there *was* a Sanctuary and we three loved it those last seven months of Glindy's life.

Looking at the Penn Avenue side of our new building; its Fisk Street side is on the right.

Chapter 7

THE SANCTUARY

It was the least likely place on our whole grounds for a Sanctuary when Glindy, Cerid and I first selected the area behind the Infirmary for our Sanctuary, thus making it sacred to us.

I would find an old crumbly tree stump to sit on. Glindy would sit beside me, and Cerid would explore and roam all over the place until sometimes we wondered where she was and if we ought to go and find her. But always she came back just in time to spare this effort. Glindy was a worry-bird like his mistress but she, Cerid, wasn't and enjoyed everything, including roaming. He was old and savored the peace of the place for he hadn't much longer to live, though none of us knew it at the time, or maybe *he* did. Cerid savored the excitement of the hideout and the privacy. Thus it became a favorite haunt with all three of us.

Officially, there was already a Sanctuary belonging to the grounds, a beautiful little chapel in the Episcopal Church Home next door, to which our building was connected on the first floor by a long corridor. Open to us apartment tenants from nine to four, the corridor was automatically closed at that hour for the Home's own privacy. I often went to the little chapel for its weekly services.

The Episcopal Church Home had been in existence since 1834 and its very age hallowed it, as did also its many priceless keepsakes of furniture and objects of art in the lovely drawing room on its first floor. These had been inherited through the years from earlier residents of the Home and Diocesan donors. The apartment tenants were privileged to enjoy the musicales and other events given in the drawing room from time to time. But of course Glindy and Cerid couldn't partake of such privileges, and we liked to enjoy things together, just the three of us.

Every day when we were out walking, we headed for our spot without discussing the matter, and there we sat down, among the tree stumps, broken sticks, stones, worn-out, discarded fence palings and tree branches, that the enclosure, being hidden on the slope behind the Infirmary, served as a catch-all for. None of the disarray bothered us in the least and actually we liked the earthy, close-to-the-soil atmosphere. There was peace, and a feeling of being close to Nature, and no one could see us, not even the schoolchildren, because they never thought of looking up at the grassy slope, and Cerid, our little family "barker" was always quiet there, as she usually was when Glindy was with her.

Sometimes Glindy would look at me, his eyes saying "thank you for this peace." I would remove his collar and leash, though there was no need to, for he never stirred once we got there. Often we would say our prayers out loud, with Cerid wandering away from prayers to the apple trees, to see if any apples had fallen. Occasionally we would hear the voices of the nurses talking to the sick ladies in the Infirmary. There was a wee garden close to it, which was like a cloister, sweet and holy. The trucks rolling up and down the hill never annoyed us in the Sanctuary, though when we were out walking on the street we called them names for being so noisy.

All this was in the olden, golden days when we were all alive and came to the apartment building when it first opened, in the summer of 1973. But Glindy, as we've already mentioned, died within seven months and that ended the golden days for us. Yes, Cerid and I went there after he left for Heaven, but there wasn't the same incentive, I being only a pal to her and he being her *ALL*, the One she couldn't live without. She grieved quietly; I did, too, but at that time and before her diabetes came, we took each other for granted. Thus the Sanctuary for a while became a less-hallowed place for she barked at the trucks, the schoolchildren and everyone else—a perfectly safe pastime, protected as she was by the high fence surrounding *all* of the grounds, not just our Sanctuary. In apple season she forgot to bark and headed straight for the apple trees to munch on fallen apples, till I thought she would burst.

When June came she *was* impressed with the Sanctuary's rose garden, and stopped often to admire the many roses. They were a riot of gorgeous colors —scarlet, salmon, pink and virgin white, with some unbelievable lemon-tinted beauties at the fence, all by themselves.

A luxuriant clump of climbing roses scaled the wall of the Infirmary building, beside which, when she was in the mood, she played hide-and-seek with me silently—for I had told her she mustn't disturb the sick ladies inside. But mostly the little Explorer was busy with discovering the secrets of the Sanctuary, and her merry little backside wove in and out of the bushes and trees with abandon, while I sat quietly on a tree stump watching her, and thinking—because Glindy was always there, in *spirit*. When she was ready to leave she would signal me, but would get so far ahead I'd have to signal *her* and yell "wait a minute," so I could catch up.

After *she* died, I still went to the Sanctuary every day for months, to feel her spirit there. Hers and Glindy's. They were always there to greet me, and I felt their presence palpably . . . keenly. The Sanctuary by then had taken on a more tidy look. How Glindy would have appreciated its greenness and orderliness! How Cerid would have revelled in the newly-leveled space to roam! Or would she? The tidiness of the place might have bored her, she being ever one for nosing about and burrowing into the rubble of the early days.

Quiet now, hardly anyone comes to the Sanctuary any more except Glindy's and Cerid's mistress, and of course the gardener and maintenance men, on their rounds. In wintertime even Mother Nature herself limits her visits, but no matter! Our spirits are always there. The lights and shadows of Eternity are there, too. See how the sun plays its rays on the old tree stump where we sat? It is the Sun's hiding-place. See how the Moon and Stars lend their radiance to envelope us and close us in with their holiness? It is their Sanctuary, as well as ours . . . .

Here we stand in our Sanctuary looking across the street. That building I have marked with an X is the United States Steel Building far and away in downtown Pittsburgh.

Ceridwen — The Wife and Mother.

PART TWO

Glindy and Cerid in their last picture together, for he died on March 28, 1974 and it was our Christmas-card 1973 picture of them.

Chapter 8

EMERGING

Always, when Glindy was alive, Cerid had played "second fiddle" in everything to him. Not in a deprecating sort of way but as though she had chosen the role, her love for him being so overwhelming it seemed *her* self was lost in his. She stepped back always so he might go in or out of the door first; she waited until he chose a place to rest; then found her rest beside him. She never started her meals until he began to eat and if there was anything left over in his dish, which usually was, he being a poor eater, she waited for the go-sign from him before touching his dish. That was her way, her wish, she was happy in it, and she took her every cue from him. Marriages, they say, are made in Heaven; theirs was, and if it had been a human marriage it would have been "a perfect union." They would have been "the perfect couple," with nothing effuse in it.

So when Glindy died, she died too, figuratively speaking. Our veterinarian always contended his death brought on her diabetes, when I questioned him later about how in the world she got it when she had never eaten candy in her life or been exposed to sweets. But gradually as the months wore on after he died, there were heartening signs that a new, more venturesome Ceridwen was emerging, or perhaps it was the early, original Ceridwen returning.

Anyway, she was acting more and more on her own initiative, and reverting to the Ceridwen of her puppy days. Of course Glindy's very name would bring her back sharply to a haunting remembrance of him, and she would stand quietly still, when he was mentioned. Then I would think of something funny to make her laugh, so we wouldn't fall into the habit of never speaking of him without sadness. I'd say "wonder what Glindy's doing now up there in Heaven? . . . I'll bet he's thinking of us, don't you?" and she would return to a gay mood.

For a long time after he left, she wandered aimlessly about the apartment, looking for him, just from habit. She clung to me more, too, becoming more attached and possessive of her mistress. Better still, she became more expansive in her relationship with others in the building, gaining confidence in herself day by day. I could always sympathize with her in mourning for him because I missed Glindy inordinately too. We comforted each other.

The months went by as the new Ceridwen was finding herself and adjusting to life without her spouse. We talked of Glindy constantly, and she listened eagerly, but often I had the feeling she expected him to come back some day, for sometimes when we discussed him there was such an expectant look on her face it was disheartening.

Day by day in every way, our lives moved on and for the next several pages here are some of the "ways," some of the things we did, never at any time forgetting Glindy.

Standing at the end of the Sanctuary, you are looking down 40th Street from the height of our walled property. That flat, grassy area adjoining the building across the street, shows a glimpse of Arsenal Park.

Chapter 9

DAY BY DAY ... IN EVERY WAY

The Miracle of the Bone

Cerid was forever picking up things on the street when we went walking and I was forever scolding her about this, and telling her about germs. She reacted to the subject of germs as if they were a funny story, and went right on picking up any old thing — whether it was part of a thrown-away sandwich, chewing gum (already chewed), rejected candy bars the school-kids had cast away — and even nuts and bolts and other hardware from passing vehicles. As long as it was bite-size, into her mouth it went, before I could reach down and grab it.

Bones of any kind were prohibited by her beloved vet, but he wasn't standing by when a nice juicy one bobbed up on the street and beckoned to Cerid invitingly. One time one of those devils got wedged between her teeth and she walked with a wooden and frantic look all the way home, stopping often to struggle with it, and try to loosen it.

Foolishly when we got home I scolded her, but it was evident she didn't need it, but *did* need all her strength (mine too) to dislodge that bone. So I shut up and we both settled down to the business of attacking it, but it refused to budge.

This was getting serious so I called the nearby vet, ours being too far away for such an emergency. It was nearing office-closing time for the nearby vet and he wasn't about to be deterred by a bone.

So we yanked and prayed and prayed and yanked, not stopping, until all at once quietly and miraculously, it just dropped easily out of her mouth; and while she was sitting there looking happily relieved, I hurriedly grabbed it before she could get any new ideas about that bone.

"Enough is enough," I told her, throwing it into the garbage can.

Sleeping with Cerid (If that's what you call it.)

It never was deep sleep with Cerid, nor had it ever been with Glindy, as it is with some dogs I've read about in the dog books. For at any hour of the day or night, with them it was simply dozing.

Not a sound sleeper myself and given to prowling around the apartment

49

in the wee hours — cautiously so as to try not to awaken them — *they* were both awake and wide-eyed, watching every move I made from their beds, hoping for a handout if I was having a snack, or a cup of coffee. After Glindy died, Cerid was lonely for him at night, his empty bed being still beside her. So I used to talk with her from my bed and tell her stories about him.

Her eyes would sympathize as she waited for me to get up and give her the expected pat on the back. Then we would both settle down in a fresh effort to go to sleep. Sound sleep eluded her all of her life and many times I'd find her already up, at the foot of my bed in the morning, having quietly climbed or jumped from her high bed without my knowing it.

Stubbornness

Stubbornness with Cerid was a point of view, not a characteristic as one might think, and naturally the point of view was hers — exclusively. She hadn't the slightest objection to *your* point of view, but please don't deny her hers, or you'll run into trouble — also lose a lot of time. She could hold out forever, and not lose her temper. You were the one that did that. Even as a puppy this trait manifested itself. Remember how she was that first day I landed in Wales and wanted her to go for a walk? Nothing doing! She squatted down in the middle of the road, refusing to budge and that was that.

Most puppies wouldn't have had the gumption, to say nothing of the courage, to hold out against the whole village. But she did, against impatient cows, sheep and honking automobiles, and carried it off without the slightest dent in her usual calm. I learned then and have tried to remember ever after, to "yield" and after a minute little Miss Cerid was doing the same. This, by the way, is a corgi trait, corgis being a proud, rugged-individualist breed, averse to subjection or coercion of any kind.

* * * * *

The Tail is not always a Barometer.

Whoever heard of a dog without a tail? Well, Cerid didn't have one, she being a Pembrokeshire corgi, though Cardiganshire corgis *do* have tails; lovely, bushy, beautiful tails, like a fox.

A dog's tail is supposed to be a barometer as to how he feels. Maybe so, but lack of a tail never hindered Cerid from showing how *she* felt. She waved her merry little backside when she was happy, and shook her head angrily displaying her front teeth when highly displeased. And when *that* happened, you'd better watch out, or she'd give you a run.

* * * * *

Arsenal Park and a Brush With History

"Say something, Cerid," I called to her one fine morning from across the room. I was making the bed, and she was sitting half-in, half-out of deep thought. "What's on your mind this beautiful day?"

She gave a couple of barks intended to mean "a walk in the park" — Arsenal Park that is, near our apartment building in the Lawrenceville section of Pittsburgh. One of the oldest parks in the city, it had an interesting history, and had figured prominently in our nation's wars. In fact that's how it got its name, having been a big arsenal for the storage of ammunition during the War of 1812.

Cerid liked walking in the park, and especially relished the sight of the big cannon at the park's entrance. The neighborhood children liked it too and climbed all over it on their way to and from school. She enjoyed their antics and often participated in the fun. When Glindy was alive he liked Arsenal Park, too, and the three of us went there for daily walks though it was a mixed pleasure for him, because big male dogs on leash taunted him, offering challenges he was too old to accept and worrisome to all of us. So we preferred the park when it was empty and timed our strolls accordingly. It was a pleasant time too when the little children played on the swings and slides, their parents watching them. Their laughter was music to our ears.

After Glindy went to Heaven, the park walks became more serene for Cerid barked so loud and long at the big male dogs passing by, they ran away. The park was a quiet restful place to sit down and the Arsenal High School students next door, with their droning lessons and lively athletic activities, were good company. We sat on the benches hours on end, she at my feet, flat on her stomach, front paws outstretched, drinking in the songs of the birds, the hum of the park's lawnmowers and the rumblings of the trucks making their way up and down Fortieth Street.

"My, that's a big one," I would say of a goliath of a truck passing by. She would raise her head to look first at the truck and then at me contentedly, during those happy days.

Sometimes I would tell her bits of stories about the park's history: "Do you know this place was the first United States *arsenal* west of the Allegheny Mountains?" I would explain. "It was a *beehive* of activity during the War of 1812. Look down there, Cerid — see that plaque on the side of the Washington Educational Building? . . . In 1753 George Washington and Colonel Christopher Gist rested right at that very spot, after crossing the Allegheny River on their way to Fort LeBouef on a dangerous mission during the Revolutionary War. Some day we'll go down and have a look at that plaque, Cerid, but not now. . . .

"By the way, did you notice that big white house on Penn Avenue yesterday when we were out walking? Well, *Stephen Foster,* Pittsburgh's beloved and world-famous songwriter, was born in that house. And his father, *Colonel William Foster,* was the man who drew up the charter in 1854 for Lawrenceville, this community in which we live. He gave it the name Lawrenceville in honor of *Captain James Lawrence,* who died defending his ship as a young naval captain in the Spanish-American War, when he was only thirty-two years old. His last words: "Don't give up the Ship" have come to be famous the world over for instilling loyalty and courage in the hearts of men facing danger. And here's something else, Cerid. . . .

"I read much of what I'm telling you in that library we just passed on our way down to the park, which by the way is the *oldest* library in the city of Pittsburgh . . .isn't that something! I always thought the library on the north side was the oldest in our city. . . . ."

After talking so much I was silent for a while to savor the park's tranquility, but not for long because *another* historical fact came to mind: "Long ago, in the year 1862, when this park was a thriving arsenal," I told her, "with hundreds of employees, a terrible explosion of gunpowder, stored in the main building, killed eighty people. The newspapers called it 'the bloodiest day in Pittsburgh history,' Cerid. . . ."

Ending the history lesson on a happier note, I mentioned *Howard Heinz,* Pittsburgh's world-famous food-industrialist, who once had owned this park in later years when it was no longer an arsenal, having bought it from the Government so he could present it to the city of Pittsburgh as a recreational facility.

. . . Summoning her attention, I said: "Look over there through the trees, Cerid, and you'll see, on the horizon, the magnificent *United States Steel Building.* Pittsburgh is called 'The Steel City' and has been the home of *many* steel magnates, among them Andrew Carnegie and the Joneses and the Laughlins; and we mustn't forget there were some famous bankers here too, like the Mellons. All of these men left their mark on Pittsburgh, Cerid, to make it the great city it is."

Pausing for breath at last *and* looking down at my little companion, I saw she was dozing happily at my feet, and suddenly realized we had been talking too long and it was nearing dinnertime. So I fastened her leash, headed for home — and that was the end of the history lesson.

Wanna Lick, Anyone?

The other day I went to a church supper, and they're supposed to be quite proper affairs, you must admit. At this one the home-cooked dinner was especially good, and after his last mouthful, the pleasant-looking man on my right smiled and said, "I wish I was home now and I'd lick this plate clean." He didn't realize everyone at the table was listening and laughed uproariously, that is everyone except his wife, and she blushed crimson. But she needn't have, because the rest of us shared his sentiments. I thought of Cerid and how she had been before she got diabetes. One of her *greatest* pleasures was "licking the plate clean," her own plate first and then mine, and lastly, the skillet the meat had been cooked in.

She'd wait patiently until I finished my supper, knowing dishwashing time would soon come when I would hand her the skillet to lick. Now this wasn't a sanitary custom, to be sure, but she got so much pleasure out of it, I closed my eyes to the unsanitary aspects and gave the skillet an extra scrubbing when she finally relinquished it, just to salve my own conscience about possible germs. Not hers.

Some nights I would get up from the table and retire to my favorite chair, unwittingly forgetting the dishes momentarily, and my little dinner companion. Then I would feel her eyes resting upon me with infinite patience, waiting for the precious skillet. Jumping up, I would apologize, and yanking it from the stove, would give it to her. She would settle down to licking the skillet with gusto, and nothing would pry her loose until every last morsel was gone.

"Horrors," some of you are thinking, and perhaps I should be thinking so, too. But I wouldn't have robbed her of that pleasure for a dozen skillets and sanitation rules, so will offer apologies to *no* one for these sentiments.

* * * * *

Cerid Liked To Have Her Picture Taken—Sometimes . . .

When Glindy was alive, he and Cerid loved to have their picture taken— that is to say Glindy did, and the minute they saw me with the camera he went to the outside door, she following him, and they were both ready to pose ad infinitum. . . . Maybe I wasn't even thinking of taking *their* picture and wanted a snapshop of our new landscaping, or some other scene. But never mind, *that* had to wait until the two little photo-conscious subjects were taken care of first. While Glindy lived, there was always their annual Christmas card, or I should say mine, for our Yuletide greeting to relatives and friends. This was a big event in their lives, but after he died Cerid didn't like to pose alone, and always looked bored, and sometimes even refused to oblige. . . .

How often I have wished we had taken a picture of her surrounded by all the nuts, bolts, bottle caps, miniature spark plugs, stogie butts, cigarette holders, woolen caps and other "collectibles" she carried home from our walks. *That* would have been a *masterpiece!*

* * * * *

There Goes the Telephone

Unlike Glindy, to whom the telephone was an everlasting nuisance, Cerid could let it ring all day unconcernedly. Except once in a while and on rare occasions, she would look up at me inquiringly, while it was ringing, her ears up tight, plainly asking "aren't you going to *answer* it?"

I never did understand why one telephone ring was different from another to her, but it was, for she had her own powers of perception.

* * * * *

Rain, Rain, Go Away

In her younger days Cerid took rain in her stride—philosophically—as she took everything else, and if I didn't watch her she would jump up on the couch soaking wet, after coming in from a downpour.

We usually used a rainfall to give her a shampoo, rainwater being soft and ideal for that purpose. That was the blessing of rain for she loved to feel clean above all else. She loved to listen to the raindrops beating against the window too, and watch them sliding down the glass. They fascinated her.

* * * * *

No Tricks or Treats

Cerid looked on tricks as beneath her dignity. She would do *anything* to oblige her mistress or a friend, but no tricks, please, and since she wasn't a show dog obliged to go through such practices (though they aren't called "tricks" in the show-ring) she escaped them. Glindy felt the same way, only more so, and the nearest he came to tricks was what we called "saying his prayers," which entailed standing on his hind legs and holding his front paws in front of him. One time when he did this unconsciously, I said "Oh you look like you're saying your prayers" and ever after that, when he felt like it, he would "say his prayers" more or less obligingly. But Cerid ignored this achievement.

The other day, while out walking in our Lawrenceville neighborhood, I stopped to admire a beautiful red Irish setter, with a gleaming coat. Appreciating my admiring looks, his master said: "Show the lady how you can get down on your back and roll over." The dog did so, halfheartedly, and performed one or two other tricks, but you could see he was only doing them to please his master. I gave the setter a pat on the back and said, "good boy," but came away feeling a little sad to see a noble animal groveling in the dust that way just to bolster the pride of his master.

* * * * *

Friends

Cerid had innumerable friends, but it was always a joy to see her racing back to her mistress for the welcoming pat-on-the-back after she had strayed too far to say hello to a friend. That was the joy of her and the comfort. She knew everyone in our apartment building — the ones who liked her and those who didn't — and never failed to greet those who did.

Some of her friends I wasn't even aware of — like the ladies in the Infirmary next door — until one day, Marty, the boy who sometimes walked her after school, asked if Cerid might visit her friends in the Infirmary. They had been waving to her right along and wanted to meet her face-to-face. Of course it was all right with me, but what about the nurses? I asked Marty. He assured me they welcomed the idea and had even suggested it. So one sunny afternoon he and Cerid went calling.

Many of the ladies were in wheelchairs and Cerid stopped gaily and politely at each chair for a word with its occupant, and a smile, before going to the next group of ladies, who were watching television. With them she showed off a little by apeing the performers, and they laughed.

When she came to the really sick ladies she was most reverent, standing by their beds and understanding perfectly she must be very quiet. She almost tiptoed (her version of it) out of their rooms and said good-bye noiselessly. So it was a successful visit and all the ladies invited her to "come back again soon, Cerid," calling her by name.

Sometimes I discovered unknown friends of hers (unknown to me) in the park or on the street as a man or woman would call from the park benches: "Hello, Cerid, where are you going?" They were evidently acquaintances she had come to know when out walking with Marty. After returning their greeting, she would look up at me as if to explain who they were.

* * * * *

Cerid Never Had Any Time For Cats

When we were out walking, if Cerid hadn't always been restrained by a leash, she would have been rough on cats, and chased them right out of town.

Usually they scooted away at the first sight of her, but occasionally one would stand up for his or her rights. Spitting with rage, and towering to twice its size, it would challenge her to a confrontation. Undaunted, Cerid would return the challenge and lunge forward with equal rage, at which point I would call a halt to the affair and tell her to let the poor cat alone.

Which brings to mind a funny story about a cat...want to hear it? It was a cat named Tobermory, after its famous namesake in one of H. H. Munro's "Saki" stories. It belonged to *Enid Beaupre,* a dear Welsh friend of my long-ago New York days, living in Forest Hills. Enid babied Tobermory without ceasing, but she needn't have, for "Toby" was in the pink of health, was quite a character, and could very well take care of himself. He had the run of the house and the "running" of Enid and he made good use of his privileges. He went everywhere with his mistress, even to the supermarket, comfortably lying in the bottom of the shopping cart, with a soft pillow beneath him, and he was the cynosure of all eyes in his neighborhood and lived in the lap of luxury, so to speak.

One day Tobermory failed to go to his litter box for the call of Nature, and there was nothing in the box to show for it. Next day the same thing happened. Obviously this can't go on, thought his mistress, or he'll get seriously sick. So Enid called the vet and arranged to take Toby to his hospital. But just as she was going out the door to the taxi, she happened to glance into the bathroom: "Oh dear, I forgot to flush that toilet again — what's the matter with me?"

The vet listened to Enid's story about Toby with concern, and examined him. Then, peevishly, so it could be heard almost to the outer office, he yelled, "What do you *mean* this cat hasn't been defacating? He defacated less than an hour ago." With that he dismissed *both* of them abruptly, calling in the next patient — a dog, at whom Toby glanced menacingly.

In a matter of minutes a taxi came to take them home, with Tobermory hurrying into the house ahead of Enid, as was his usual wont. She hung her coat and hat in the hall cupboard, then sat down in her rocking chair for a brief rest.

After a while she felt the call of Nature herself and headed for the bathroom where she had the surprise of her life. There, astride the commode seat, as nice as could be, was Tobermory! She couldn't believe her own eyes. Of course he scrambled down to his litter box fast enough and yielded his perch to Enid.

She called the vet to tell him about it and you could have heard him laughing all the way from Forest Hills to Manhattan. Tobermory by this time was hiding under the bed, being uncertain as to the outcome of the affair.

Enid, however, soon put a stop to his newest achievement, which Tobermory didn't appreciate at all; and he pouted for almost a week.

* * * * *

Cerid, The Serene

There was always a serene Cerid, even as a puppy. Most of us look on serenity as a rare virtue reserved for queens, saints, philosophers and the like, and seldom associate it with dogs. But Cerid had it, and it wasn't a passive trait either, for it came to the fore always when needed, and was there, like an invisible cloak wrapped around her. . . .

* * * * *

An Odd Sort of Jail

Never long on discipline with either Glindy or Cerid, I sometimes learned how to "cope" in curious ways. For instance when Cerid's monumental stubbornness got completely out of hand, I sent her to the bathroom — yes, the *bathroom* — for punishment, the most unlikely place in the whole apartment for incarceration. I guess she hated being alone with all those white, shiny objects around, and it was real punishment to her. The joke of it, too, was she could easily have eased her way out, for the door wasn't ever completely shut, to let in a little air. But she would never have thought of escaping, this being an example of what I have always called "corgi *honor.*" She, believing she deserved the punishment, was *willing* to take what was coming to her.

Sometimes I attempted to smack her, but this became a game, and I ended up smacking the wall instead. So it was no punishment. At the end of my patience I would say: "All right then . . .BATHROOM!" after a big argument. She would go there meekly as a lamb and stay "behind bars" with Glindy peeking in and splitting his sides laughing, until I thought she had had enough punishment, and would tell her to come out. She came, hanging her head in shame.

* * * * *

Teasing was her middle name

There never was a time when Cerid wasn't a compulsive tease, even from her puppy days. When we were readying to go walking, she would usually watch me gathering up my coat, hat, galoshes, gloves, et cetera, if it was wintertime, plus her leash and collar; and, just as we were about to take off, she would grab something, maybe my hat or a glove and chase around the room with it, with me after her. Sometimes I would get angry and tell her off, thinking the scolding was sinking in, but no fear, when she looked her saintliest a new smirk would come over her face and she ran to the bathroom to grab a towel drying on the towel rack.

"You're *not* taking that turkish towel for a walk," I would scream, by this time loud enough for everyone on our floor to hear and think I was demented, until they saw us both emerging into the hall, the towel tightly clutched in her mouth, with me pulling at it. One time the cleaning-lady playfully tossed her a duster, and in a minute they were both involved in the tug-of-war game of their lives.

When it was freezing weather she would snatch my gloves and run to our apartment door with them. In fact anyone's gloves were fair game to her, and many a glove owner waiting for the elevator was jolted out of a quiet reverie by Cerid's quick snatching of his or her gloves. Some of them laughed, others didn't appreciate the joke. So I warned everyone to pocket their belongings when they saw Cerid coming.

She was a tease about playing ball, too, and always accepted the invitation when someone threw the ball to her. But more often than not, the thrower was thwarted and the game was ended before it began by Cerid's forcible possession of the ball.

Occasionally I wasn't in the mood for these going-for-a-walk-shenanigans and would sit down on a nearby chair and say: "All right, we just won't go for a walk now" and pretend to take my coat off. Her playful mood would change immediately and she was the soul of contriteness. Putting her head between my knees, she would *beg* for forgiveness. Then, with me feeling like a "heel," we both headed for the great outdoors, chastened momentarily.

* * * * *

Susie

Susie was the dog across the hall from us, and she and Cerid were the best of friends. That nonsense about strange dogs not getting along together never entered Susie's and Cerid's heads.

When they first met, though, Susie was the shyer dog of the two. They sized each other up nose-wise, shook themselves all over approvingly, and were friends ever after. Just like that!

Susie was a mixed collie and had the beautiful collie face, with eyes full of love and concern for her mistress. Those eyes followed Monica, her mistress, adoringly, as she went about their apartment like the old-lady-who-lived-in-the-shoe, in the nursery rhyme; for Monica had unsteady feet and was always falling. For that reason she couldn't ever take Susie for a walk, so a neighborhood friend came and took Susie out walking daily.

Actually, Susie barked more than Cerid, but this was not to her discredit, for Cerid had plenty to say too, and it was well she and Susie were loyal to each other, for no one else was especially mindful of them except their two mistresses, until they did something wrong and then they got *plenty* of attention.

All this was how it was in the early days when the apartment had just opened and the handful of tenants, who were dog lovers, were allowed to bring them. Nowadays, dog owners are *not* permitted to rent apartments in our building. More's the pity, too, for they always seem to add permanence to a structure.

Sometimes Susie came to call on Cerid. They were precious together — very polite during a visit, not making a single error of behavior until perhaps Cerid got the notion that I was being *too* polite to Susie, and would give me a meaningful nudge by way of saying, "I'm here, too." Whereupon I would pat and praise the both of them inordinately, using both hands.

Susie's mistress was just as fond of Susie as I was of Cerid and she and I were willing to discuss our dogs with any or all of the other tenants who would listen, and we were always worrying about what was going to happen to Susie and Cerid when we were no more, and exchanging comforting thoughts about this. But we never told anyone Cerid's and Susie's secrets. The secret I liked best about *Susie* was what she always had for breakfast, when she sat down to eat with her mistress first thing in the morning. She was infinitely polite and had wonderful table manners as she partook of her toast, with butter on, cereal (with milk), sometimes an egg, and here's the secret: *ALWAYS COFFEE.* Who liked coffee better — Susie or her mistress? No one could say for sure, because they both had a passion for it that was good to see. Susie drank her coffee from a saucer, of course, and with relish; but neither of them cared a hoot whether it was good for their systems or not. Though there certainly was no doubt *ever,* about its being good for their souls!

* * * * *

Apropos of Dog Ownership — A Credo

I have never said and thought, I am a *dog owner,* either relating to Glindy *or* Cerid, except for accepting responsibility for their actions. For I believe no living creature has the right to "own" another, be it dog or man. It is an abhorrent thought, since a dog's life — *any* life — is a "gift" from the Creator Himself; without strings attached and uniquely given to *all* living creatures. In *that* sense, no one can *rightfully* think or say he *owns* another be it dog or man.

* * * * *

"Her Bark Was Worse Than Her Bite"

Actually no one ever felt Cerid's bite, to know whether it was better or worse than some one else's, because she never bit anyone in her life. But everyone within range of hearing, at one time or another, tasted her bark. She barked on principle, and for reasons fully known to her, though not always apparent to others. This doesn't refer to her joyful barks, for they had a pleasant "taste" and were good for the soul.

One time shortly after her arrival in America, we were all sitting on our front porch in Edgewood, enjoying the cool breezes after a hot summer day. A woman walked by on the street and all at once Cerid started barking at that woman loudly. Glindy and I hadn't the faintest idea what the woman had done to deserve such a bawling out, but *Cerid* knew. After she got through with the barking, she shook her shoulders vigorously and delivered a final bark, and believe it or not, it sounded like *"Humpf"* plain as could be!

With her everlasting good nature her barking was usually just plain bluffing, for she wouldn't have known what to do if other dogs *had* followed through and called her bluff. One time when she was walking in Arsenal Park with her friend Marty, a big Irish setter confronted them, and she barked at him so loudly and long the huge dog got rattled and ran away, never stopping to see if she was after him or not.

* * * * *

Cerid, the Inscrutable. . . (that Look!)

Sometimes as I sat reading in my favorite chair, I would feel Cerid's eyes riveted upon me, from the farthest corner of the room, and this discomfited me. Putting down the book, I would say: "What are you looking at, Cerid?" a trifle playfully, to rout her seriousness.

There was no answer, but after a moderate pause she would resume looking, almost searchingly, the way animals look, and see things invisible to the human eye. The look continued to puzzle me, but at last I would return to the book, still conscious of the mute search in her eyes.

I would call her to me once, twice, thrice, before she would come shyly, and lie at my feet. Stroking and patting her on the back, with her nudging me for more, finally there was enough affection to reassure her. Then, and only then, would she close her eyes and relax. What in the world had she been worrying about, I wondered?

Demonstrative affection was vital to Cerid, more so than to Glindy. Sometimes I forgot this. Then came that hungry look. Other times her eyes would just rest on me as though savoring our relationship and presence together.

Even when we were out walking, she would often stop, turn around, and look at me questioningly. Not being able to divine the question in her eyes, I was helpless to give the answer. This made both of us sad.

* * * * *

Sometimes A Teacher . . .

When she died, our veterinarian said that in a way Cerid had taught him how to live. It was a wholly spontaneous remark and somewhat surprised me, but it made me realize that she had taught me some lessons, too — like how to laugh when I felt like crying; how to sit quietly when in the foggiest dither; how to say, "I'm sorry" graciously, when occasion suggested it, and I didn't want to.

She was a teacher with a vast *"uncommon"* common sense and an unparalleled flair for diplomacy.

That's what the vet meant when he said she taught him how to live.

* * * * *

Lose something, Esther?

Whenever I got a cold, mislaid my keyes or glasses (the latter about every hour or so) it aroused Cerid's sympathy inordinately. Her face awash with concern, she followed me around the room everywhere, until I found the lost article and all was well again.

My keys had an everlasting habit of disappearing and a search set in, with her dogging my footsteps as I hunted. Male-like, Glindy took no notice of such feminine foibles, except to peer occasionally from the corner of his eye to see how the search was going. From long experience he knew how it would *end*.

He was good-humored, however, about my glasses. They *did* interest him and he had even worked out a system for their disappearances, which was nothing more than watching where I put them. Then after a spell with Cerid and me hunting everywhere, he would arouse himself and wander over amiably to *exactly* where they were and wait self-consciously for my pat on the back and flattering praises. If they were right *on* my eyes and face, and I was unaware of this, he would merely look *up* at my face (to point to them).

But poor little Cerid suffered with her mistress every time things got lost and wasn't happy until she heard the familiar squeal of discovery, "Oh, *here* they are, Cerid, come look!"

* * * * *

Cerid and Music

Cerid liked music, no question about it. Maybe not rock music with its turbulence and noise; or boopa-doop, thumpy music (noisy, too), though when Glindy was alive he could drown those boopa-doop boys out of business any time he wanted to. Country music? Well, Cerid could take it or leave it — it made no impression either way. But give her a catchy tune on TV, or soothing music, or maybe a hymn, and you had her! Up went her ears like antennas and she would stop anything she was doing to listen, standing so close to the television set you were afraid she might get an electrical shock of some kind.

Yet, much as she liked music she never participated in it like Glindy did. He used to sing along with the artists and help them if he thought they needed it. But *her* pleasure was in listening and if a song was sung to her satisfaction, she retired to her corner and savored it before settling down to a bit of a snooze.

Often I would break into a song to rouse her spirits after Glindy went to Heaven. She loved this, and taking a position at my feet would listen with all her might until the last verse was sung. "Home On The Range" was a favorite and Eugene Field's "There Little Girl Don't Cry" rated high on her list of favorites too because she always imagined herself to be the little girl in the song. "The Old Gray Goose Is Dead," a favorite of *my* childhood, was in our repertoire, though its tune long-forgotten was easily improvised as we went along:

Go and tell Aunt Peggy; go and tell Aunt Peg—gg—gy
Go and tell Aunt Peggy The Old Gray Goose Is Dead. . .

The one that she's been saving; The one that she's been sav—vv—ing
The one that she's been saving; to make a feather bed.

It was a good song and we sang it with feeling. After we had duly notified Aunt Peggy and sufficiently mourned the loss of her old gray goose we felt we had done all we could and usually took a rest, being worn-out.

Sunday School hymns were always popular: "Throw Out the Lifeline" was one of them, and we threw out that lifeline to those poor shipwrecked seamen for all we were worth. "Precious Name," an old gospel hymn, held her spellbound, with its lovely lilting cadences and the close rapport there always is between singer and song in a good gospel hymn.

It was a pity our little reed organ never came to mind as a consolation piece for our grief after Glindy died. *He* had listened to it by the hour when I played hymns to cheer *him* up, and it might have been a comfort to Ceridwen and me. But strangely, in our befuddled, grief-stricken minds we never thought of it.

* * * * *

Dogs are not meant for apartments, and vice versa

Everyone agrees, dog lover and dog hater alike, that an apartment is no place for a dog. But we were here in our new apartment, in the Lawrenceville section of Pittsburgh, and it had to be home for the three of us. Glindy and Cerid had been superb about accepting it and settling down. The least I could do was to try to emulate them.

Over the years, the happiest home for all three of us had been our hillside home in Banksville, with the fenced-in yard, giant-sized porch and other conveniences. Although, perhaps the happiest home for Glindy *himself*, was our Edgewood abode. For Cerid, a happy home was anywhere Glindy was. But, since she was the barker of the family and made good use of her talent, there came a time when the Edgewood neighbors were unhappy about it and we moved to Banksville, to a house where there were no neighbors near enough to be discomforted. Looking back on it all now, we treasure those six years of tranquility in Banksville as one of our most precious memories.

As already related, Glindy didn't have to submit to apartment-living long, having gone to Heaven seven months after we moved to Lawrenceville. Ceridwen, a more gregarious creature than he, had made up readily with her housemates and this stood us in good stead, when apartment life was sometimes rugged. Dog lovers, in our building, were never plentiful and for every dog lover there were two dog *haters,* so life wasn't exactly sunshine and roses for little Cerid. But she took things in stride and was always a "lady," even when slurs came her way and she was blamed for things she didn't do.

Good friends, however, sometimes did rally to her support and I'll never forget one of them. This good and kind woman was sitting in the foyer with a group of other tenants, one day, as Cerid and I passed by. Someone in the group made a derogatory remark, evidently meant for Cerid, but I didn't catch it. Cerid's friend stood up and said out loud for everyone to hear:

"Well, if you ask *me*, the dogs in this building know how to behave better than the people" and walked away from the group.

The apartment grounds too were a pleasure. Surrounded by a tall iron-fence and hedges, beautifully landscaped and protected from the hurly-burly of traffic and noise on the street outside, Cerid knew every bush and tree and felt confident to roam about and explore, without interruption. Sometimes a tenant would come outdoors to go to the mailbox, or to catch a bus outside our gate, and she would always raise her head to see who it was and greet him or her, if it happened to be one of her friends.

* * * * *

Chapter 10

THE STORY OF HER STRUGGLE WITH DIABETES

The Shock

When Ceridwen was about nine years old, diabetes hit her and plagued her the rest of her life. She had been drinking water inordinately for a couple of days but was obviously well and active otherwise. This wasn't enough of an ailment for a long, expensive cab trip to our vet, who now—by our recent move to a new Senior Citizens' apartment—was at the opposite end of Pittsburgh from where we *had bee*n living, close to his hospital. Anyway, I expected the thirst habit to soon pass; but when it continued to the third day and she was beginning to look bloated, I took her to the nearest dog clinic to find out what was the matter.

Right away the veterinarian there said it was serious whatever it was, and he wasn't sure. He suggested she needed a more extensive examination than his clinic — chiefly an advisory one — was able to give and told me to to get her to her own vet as soon as possible. Next day, May 12, 1975, we went to our own vet—"Doc"—as we and everybody else called him.

They greeted each other like the old friends they were, and when he wanted her to stay overnight at his hospital for tests, and she was so plainly willing, there was nothing else for me to do so I left her there, by this time really worried.

He telephoned next day to say "Cerid," as he always called her had diabetes and had it badly; adding that it probably had been working on her for some time, and she would have to be hospitalized for another full week for tests and much-needed bloodwork. He further stated that she would have to return to the hospital every three months for the rest of her life for these tests and bloodwork. Up to then I thought he was making a mountain-out-of-a-molehill, but with this kind of talk I was astounded.

A week later, he phoned to say I could take Cerid home but he definitely wanted me to have a talk with him before she could be released, then made an appointment for the next day. Poor little Cerid—what was this all about? Thinking about it kept me awake all night.

The next day, I sat across from him in a state of shock as he gravely unfolded the facts about Cerid's illness, she lying at his feet taking it all in good-humoredly. It was as if he were talking about someone else the whole time.

It sounded so sudden and unreal. Diabetes, he said, in her advanced state, would require daily insulin injections. That was Point One. Point Two: She must be put —*and kept* —on a rigid diet, to keep the disease under control. Point Three: As he had already intimated, she must be brought to his hospital *religiously* every three months, for the much-needed examinations and tests.

She looked so well and contented there beside him that I argued: it must be a mistake. But no, it wasn't. His seriousness began to get hold of my befuddled brain. I kept telling him I couldn't handle all this, and wouldn't, shuddering at the thought of sticking a needle full of insulin into Cerid's body every day. He wasted no time persuading me, saying, "Yes, you can, and *will.* I have confidence in you." Then ringing a buzzer for one of the attendants, he told her to show me the injection procedure and left the room.

Cerid and I were both trembling as the girl put us through the procedure, explaining how to hold the needle, how to measure the insulin (by units), where to thrust it into her body (the best, muscle-free places and so on). Then working with water first, she made me try it and stood by watching as I fearfully, prayerfully, gave Cerid the water injection. Later came the actual "shot," which initially was in the low twenties as to number of units, but soon increased and did so ever after. Cerid was an angel through the whole ugly procedure and I grabbed her after it was over in a big hug saying, "Oh, honey, we made it — we *made* it." But my mind was a complete blank.

Next, the urinalysis procedure was explained. It was a first-thing-in-the-morning ritual, and had to be done with little lengths of sensitized tape, pulled from a small tape-roll she gave me. The tape lengths were to be dipped into Cerid's urine, to register the amount of blood sugar in her blood, and were to be watched daily for any irregularities. This sounded like an anticlimax after the "shot," but I didn't realize that its worst was yet to come. Finally, the girl outlined the brief instructions about diet control. At last the whole painful interview was over and Cerid and I could go home. She was as joyful as could be.

Never having given a thought in Doc's office as to how I was going to handle the urinalysis problem *outdoors,* where Cerid always went first thing every morning for her "exercises," that matter bobbed up immediately when we got home. So I telephoned the attendant and had some more bad news. Very sweetly and without the slightest hesitation, she asked: "Haven't you got a tin cup or something you can use?"

"I guess I can find one," I answered ungraciously.

"Then hold it under Cerid as she urinates; dip the tape in it after you both get back *indoors,* if you want to. That's all there is to it."

I thought, "*What next?* . . . doesn't she realize there are more than two hundred people in this apartment building — that's four hundred eyes *look-*

ing at us and our antics! She doesn't have to do it, *that's* why she's so nice about it!' "

Next morning, bright and early, we started the tin-cup-routine, using a kitchen measuring cup, both of us squatting. After Cerid caught on to what was wanted, she performed admirably. Then when it was over, from nervousness, we both laughed loudly and irreverently — they could have heard us all over the building. Actually, it was an insanely comical routine, but didn't deserve all *that* irreverence. What the people in the building must have thought, I didn't dare imagine.

Each day, after the dippings, dipped-tape in hand, I gave Cerid the report: "Hooray, it's a nice bright yellow, that's good Cerid, and means no blood sugar"; or if it wasn't, I'd announce dolefully, "Oh, it's a St. Patrick's day green" (which meant the presence of some blood sugar, but not too much). Often, when the report was glaringly bad, I'd say with a sigh: "Oh, it's a deep, dark-brown color, the tape is, and we'll have to call the doctor and tell him." She always listened patiently to the report.

This tin-cup-ritual came to be known as her "exercises" day by day and the whole odd procedure became a game, which Cerid played cheerfully and with dignity always; and she became a wonderful sportsman. Sometimes, when she could hardly wait for the tin cup, she'd get ahead of me and I'd say: "Hey, you're ahead of me" and she'd wait patiently until that blasted tin cup was positioned properly. In this she was a Champion of the Champions and would have won trophies and blue ribbons, had there been some, and soon our fellow-apartment-dwellers came to ignore us, either disgustedly, or sympathetically, as was their wont. Some even avoided us, saying diabetes was contagious — which it isn't — and the urinalysis problem came to be no problem at all, as the girl in Doc's office had prophesied.

But the *strict diet* routine was a different matter and *was* a daily heartache because Cerid enjoyed eating above all else, as most diabetics do. After being well into a year of the disease, Doc put her on a special formula, prepared for diabetic dogs by one of the animal foundations. It was a loathsome-looking mix, resembling animated putty and came in one-pound cans, half of which Cerid was to be given in the morning and the other half at night, following her insulin shot. The wonder of it was: the ever-hungry Cerid always ate it without complaint. But she begged to sit with me later as I ate *my* supper, and *this* was the heartache, with her watching and savoring vicariously every bite that went into my mouth.

Somehow, in the months that followed, we learned how to give the shots, the food and the urinalysis perfectly, knowing her precious life depended upon it. She was wonderful through it all the next twenty-three months of her life until she died, though it wasn't easy for either of us. I guess all diabetics learn these sad lessons, but it was hard-learning for a little dog. We *learned, too, that the cure* for diabetes then and still is, even now, far into the future; which seems strange with all the progress there has been made in the field of medicine.

The Shot

There *was* a blessing, however, with our sorrow: for Cerid's and my sweetest, closest times together ever after, came to be insulin time. "Sweet," because she always was, and never became mean or angry about the shot ordeal, though the needle must surely have hurt her. I could tell this by her reactions, no matter how cautiously and gently I thrust it in.

"Close," because her illness, especially the insulin routine, removed us from the rest of the world and closed us in with our misery in a somewhat holy, private "communion." I say "our" because I never learned to be professional about it, and felt the injections as much as she did. Yet neither of us flinched when its time came. Our empathy reminds me of a childhood memory I still have of diabetes. My mother and I were coming home from church one Sunday with a fellow parishioner who, all the way home, had been telling us about the trials and tribulations of her diabetes.

After the three of us parted, I asked my mother, childlike, "Does *Mr.* Taylor have diabetes, too?" "Oh yes," replied my mother, spoofing me a bit, "he has *sympathetic* diabetes." I remember thinking, "Oh, how awful," being sure *his* kind of diabetes was even worse than his wife's. Which is sometimes the case, for often the family of a diabetic is as deeply involved in the disease as the victim himself.

"Medicine!" I would loudly announce to Cerid when time came for the shot, and the prescribed number of units of insulin were safely inside the syringe needle. She would come plodding to the couch, stepping up on her little hand-stool without a murmur. Once comfortable, just to make conversation I would say appealingly: "What shall it be tonight — right away? — or do we feel like fooling around a bit first?" making both propositions sound equally inviting.

"Fooling-around" meant she needed comforting that night and wanted me to hold her tight, calling her "the best Cerid in the whole world" and even tickling her a bit, before plunging the blasted needle in. If it was a *no-*fooling night, she would stand straight, bracing herself for the needle, a tower of self-control and strength as it went in. And oh, what rejoicing there would be when the ordeal was over, either way. We both became dizzy with joy, laughing, talking and hugging inordinately — she eager for more and more praises, until I would suddenly remember, "Oh, what about your drink of *water*?", that always being the reward after the shot, for she was ever a thirsty little one.

With that she would jump down from the couch and head for the pan of water and drink greedily. Sometimes, when her water-intake had been too high for the day, the reward would be only ice-cubes because they held less volume of water, and took longer to consume. Times when she was normally thirsty, the pan of water stood handily by, always ready for her use. When she seemed to be drinking too much, I'd say: "You'll *burst*" and she would stop immediately.

The Soldier

"Old Soldiers never die — they only fade away . . . " (From "War Song," British Army, 1914-1918.)

It was Sunday morning, March 6, 1977, almost two years since Cerid's diabetes had hit us. During all that time she had been going back and forth to the vet for regular quarterly stays of a week or more for bloodwork, check-ups, tests and so on, plus occasional trips for momentary flareups. Her insulin-intake had been fluctuating constantly, climbing upwards some days, moderating or decreasing other days, according to her condition, until by now she was on thirty units or more of insulin consistently. This seemed a walloping amount for a little dog and worried me but I could see she needed it, for her whole physical being sagged or maintained its natural rhythm from the insulin intakes. You could be guided, too, by how she looked, which was not at all like the fast-moving, lively Cerid of old, but more like an old soldier that had been through too many battles and was tired. The gay little Cerid was still gay, but with a decided effort, and, as the months went on, was more and more ready to sit quietly and just relax.

She had just come home from Doc's hospital that first week in March, after one of her umpteen trips there. We had had a perfect week together and she was glad to be home. One could see, in her gladness, glimpses of her old self again, though, understandably, she was weak. But she enjoyed our walks, watched everything that went on in our apartment building, and loyally greeted her old friends. She and I were especially chummy. It was like old times and, oh, how I hoped it would last!

Then came Sunday, that fateful seventh day of the week.

Always, this day, there were my weekly visits to my invalid sister in a nursing home some distance away; a ritual which she and Glindy, through the years, had come to expect and watch for. She attentively observed my preparations for the four-hour trip with interest, but when I took her out for her "exercises" before leaving, her stool showed a sudden change, indicating there was something amiss inside of her. These changes often came and went and I was pressed for time, so I gave her the breakfast formula as usual and hurried to catch the bus, hoping all would be normal again when I would get back; and it seemed to be, upon my arrival home. Therefore, I went about the household chores and prepared supper.

She wanted her supper (the other half-can of the formula) and ate it with relish. However, a couple of hours later, she vomited for no apparent reason and the vomiting continued on-and-off the rest of the evening, with alternate bouts of diarrhea. This was serious, and her poor little wracked body got so weak she could hardly stand up. As it was Sunday (the vet's day off at the hospital), I couldn't phone him to report the upset until the following morning, and didn't want to call anyone of the hospital staff for fear they'd say: "Bring her here for an examination,") and she would be disappointed at not finding Doc there. Besides they would have been forced to keep her overnight, to find out anything, so I decided to wait for the morning and call at nine, when "Doc" would be sure to be there.

She went outdoors for a short walk when the time came. and later submitted to the insulin injection with never-failing fortitude. But when bedtime came, no power on earth, no pleading, no prayer, could induce her to get into her own bed. So we both stretched out wearily, she on the carpet covered with newspapers, and I on top of my own bed, fully clothed, to wait out the night. Ominously, by daylight she had begun to hemorrhage. Once or twice before, since being afflicted with diabetes she had hemorrhaged briefly, but not like this. I was scared. So was she, and she had become so weak she couldn't even sip water —Water, the Elixir of her life, which she had always gulped down greedily, sick or well.

In the early morning hours we went outdoors for her exercises but came right back in without taking the urinalysis test, feeling it was presently useless, after which we settled down to the three-hour wait till nine a.m. when we could call her beloved "Doc." When it came, he was already feverishly busy with emergency surgery and told us to be at the hospital by two p.m. — he would be tied up until then.

During the rest of the morning, Cerid clung to me as though not willing to let me out of her sight, for both of us dreaded another parting. Always before going to the doctor we had made a little game out of "looking pretty," which I didn't suggest this time because of her condition. But she kept looking at me expectantly as if I was forgetting something and when she saw the brush in my hand I knew she wanted to "look pretty." It was a good sign, so I gave her a light going-over.

By now, she was hemorrhaging constantly and there was blood everywhere. We both looked helplessly at the pools of it. Her eyes were wells of fright. I never stopped holding her and praying, this being soothing and comforting for both of us.

Leave-time finally came and I called a cab. The driver, a nice young man, looked at her sympathetically. I said, "This little girl has never thought or done a mean thing in her life, but she's sick now — would you be afraid to carry her to your cab? I just can't somehow, and she's too weak to walk!"

For an answer he picked her up immediately, and *gently*, saying, "What's the matter, honey, we'll take you to the doctor, and *he'll* fix you up all right." I jumped into the back seat, a folded blanket on my lap and he took a second blanket to wrap her, and placed her, blanket and all, on my lap.

It was a 45-minute ride to the vet's hospital, no matter how you figured it. It had always been a somewhat sad journey, but this was the saddest. She sat contentedly on my lap, every now and then sidling-up close and looking at me, then turning to look out the window with interest, for she had always loved to "go for a ride." The cab driver and I didn't talk much and we rode uneventfully until coming out of the Liberty Tubes, the halfway point of our journey.

Then all at once and with a great effort she lifted her head very high, raised her body and looked out the window once more, as if she knew it was for the last time. Then she sank back onto the blanket. Next, she gave three short coughs, as if about to throw up. I tried to ease the exertions by holding her head, but it dropped limply in my hands; her jaw fell — and she became terribly quiet.

Beseeching the driver, I yelled, "Can you stop a minute — I think she's fainted or something — I can't feel her breathing either — do you think she's dead?"

"Oh, don't say such things," he yelled back impatiently. "I can't look now because we're heading into a tricky traffic jam, but I'll look in a minute." There was no further opportunity to look *or* talk as we maneuvered in and out of one traffic dilemma after another all the rest of the way to the hospital. Cerid was *still* terribly quiet on my lap.

It was only quarter to two when we reached the hospital, but we barged right through the waiting room filled with dogs and their owners, the cab driver with Cerid limp in his arms, and he looked neither to the right or left of him. Since everybody in the inner office knew me, and Ceridwen even better, they admitted us without question and watched as he placed her inert form on the nearest examining table. Washing his bloodied hands sadly, he told me how sorry he was that she was dead, and then, almost crying, left.

One of the staff veterinarians rushed in, in an attempt to revive her, but it was too late. Her heart had definitely stopped and would never beat again. He left the room, and Cerid and I were alone — together — for our last time. Her eyes were still open, so I talked with her as usual. Holding her right paw, I told her that now she was going to be with Glindy, in Heaven, where I would join them both later. Always before, she had come running into Doc's office, talking her head off. Now, not even Doc could hear her.

When he came in ten minutes, I said defensively: "Well, you didn't *have* to put her to sleep — she took care of that herself, and I'm thankful," fighting back the tears. With a vast sigh, he said: "Yes, and I'm thankful, too. You don't know *how* thankful, for I could see her getting worse every time she came here, knowing the end was bound to come soon, but I couldn't deny her the life that was left to her. She was always so alive, so full of fun, so good-natured even in the hospital that I was a *rank coward* about putting her to sleep." Then, looking away as if remembering, he said: "That little Cerid taught me how to *live!*" and laid his hands affectionately on her inert body.

Turning at last, abruptly, to face me, his whole body tired and over-wrought from hours of surgery, and seeing me by then wallowing in tears, something snapped inside of him, and he hurled these words at me: "Well, you had her for years — you *enjoyed* her, didn't you? — now what *more* do you want of her?"

This brought me sharply to my senses for I could see I deserved the re-proach and was dishonoring Cerid with my behavior. So we both stood there quietly, looking at her serene, peaceful body for a long minute in a last farewell.

Then he gently closed her eyes, which, surprisingly, were still open, and in almost a whisper he said: "I'll bury her with my own dogs," and briskly opened the outer door for me to depart, and for him to return to surgery.

I called after him as he left: "Thank you, Doc, for burying her, and for always loving her." Then, giving her a good-bye pat, I departed, too.

It was a four-block walk to the bus stop, but I wanted more walking, more time to think, being loath to go home without her. So I walked miles through that part of Pittsburgh's South Hills, until it was almost dark. It was Monday, March 7, 1977, and in another five months Cerid would have been eleven years old, if it hadn't been for diabetes.

* * * * *

DIABETES had begun to show its effects in this picture in her eyes, and towards the end of her life they even became more disfigured. Sometimes dogs AND people go blind from diabetes.

Chapter 11

THE SHELTER AND ITS HEALING GRACE

When Cerid went to the other world, aside from grief, there was an aching emptiness and uselessness about my life that nothing seemed to fill. I had been involved with dogs for seventeen years, and these years had been the happiest, most meaningful years of my life and retirement. There was some comfort in the thought that I knew she was tired of the misery and frustration of diabetes and wanted to be relieved of it. Then, too, in a way I felt she had even chosen her time and place of dying when she lay for her last hour on my lap, always a haven of contentment and peace for her since puppy days. Animals, if they have a choice, return to some special haunt for their last hour on earth before dying, knowing their time and end has come, and accepting this with more dignity than we humans.

The shock and grief of her departure was different from Glindy's, for then she had remained behind for my comfort and companionship. Now there was no one, no compulsory daily outings for walks and "exercises," no loving care and devotion to be expended on another, no sharing of experiences — in other words, nothing to keep me going. Thus, if it hadn't been for her death I might never have gone to the local animal shelter a month or so after she died. But one day, just on the spur of the moment when passing by, I dropped in and signed up as a Volunteer, selecting Tuesday for my "day at the Shelter."

The following Tuesday saw the beginning of one of the most rewarding experiences I've ever had, "my big day of the week." I became "hooked," as the saying goes, on dogs, not just Glindy and Cerid, but all dogs and was resolved to make life pleasant — particularly for the homeless dogs and cats at the Shelter.

Our Shelter was located in one of the busiest commercial sections of Pittsburgh and, unfortunately, had no outside quarters for the exercising and recreation of its occupants. That's where the Volunteer fitted into the picture and was needed for dog-walking, dog-bathing, games and the like. Despite its lack of outdoor space, however, the Shelter people managed very well with the space they did have, and were all unanimously kind to animals. It was a religion with them that they loved animals individually and collectively. Good food and loving care were never lacking. The dogs and cats had come from various sources to the Shelter. Some were lost or abandoned on

75

the city streets; some were brought by owners too ill or too old, or otherwise unable to take care of them. Some of the poor, shivering little animals were there, too, for protection, having been treated so cruelly by their owners they were brought to the Shelter by the humane authorities, or the Police. For some of the newborn puppies and kittens, the Shelter was the only home they had ever known. It welcomed them all, cats and dogs alike, and did its best to find new homes for them even though it often took months to do so. At the Shelter the animals learned that people *could* be kind, and there they need have no fear of mistreatment.

Volunteering was hard work, I soon found out, and one not only had to have the desire for it, but the physique. I learned also that truly-mean dogs are a rarity, all animals being friendly when you get to know them. They greeted me enthusiastically every Tuesday, for it meant a walk to at least half a dozen of them, as they had their turns. Nursing the puppies wasn't work at all, but sheer delight. All of us enjoyed playing with them; and I thought of the book written some years ago, entitled "Happiness Is A Warm Puppy." The girl who wrote that book *knew* what she was talking about!

Of course the dogs and cats were all confined to cages and therefore overly active when they were let out. They didn't know *how* to slow down when they got outdoors and were taken for a walk. The cats endured confinement better; and everyone there, cats and dogs alike, had a communal interest in the place, and a lively, alert watchfulness about everything that went on.

I'll never forget Trixie, my best friend there for several weeks until she was adopted. Most of the dogs were of mixed breeds and Trixie's mix I don't remember now, but it was a good one, and she was a fine dog. The minute I stood in front of her cage, she became transfixed with anticipation for her forthcoming walk. The knowledge made her almost collapse until the attendant released her for her outing. Then she would leap from the height of her double-decker cage as we got going — *really* going.

The soul of affection, everything about Trixie was young and exuberant, which I wasn't, but we got along fine and she did something that endeared her to me so much I have never forgotten it. None of the other dogs ever did it. When she was safely back in her cage after the walk, she leaned out and gave me two meaningful, loving licks on my hand, thank-you's they were, for the walk, and she never *forgot* to do this.

Then there was Nicky, an 18-months-old toy collie and terrier mix. Though a male, Nicky was much like Trixie in appearance and pep, and he was a real "pal" of a dog. My! how he savored the adventure of a walk! Nicky had a passion for movement, and we really moved — not as you're thinking, over hill and dale, as should have been, but cobblestones and more cobblestones on city streets, some almost as big as the Pyramids. Nicky and I were both well-tuckered-out after a walk.

"Taffy," a poodle-and-terrier mix, was another favorite. Taffy was a lady, no doubt about it, with a taste for the great open spaces, and a distaste for such things as cages, so that as soon as I opened her cage door she made a dash for the outside door, not waiting for me to affix her leash. Nothing, no one, could break her of this habit and there was no use trying to; but she did have a sense of honor, for she waited at the door for me to take care of the leash. Because of her exuberance and restlessness, she was sometimes housed in one of the big cages in the back room of the Shelter that I playfully dubbed: "The Civic Arena," in honor of Pittsburgh's big and beautiful sports arena of the same name.

The Shelter's "Civic Arena" had one big back door to the street and Taffy's cage was in the Arena one hot summer day at her walk-time. Forgetting that the door was momentarily open for ventilation, I was aghast as she headed for it. The lure of the open-spaces was too much for her sense of honor *that* day and she took off and was racing up and down the street before anyone could catch her. Soon all of us were involved in the roundup, when she at last was "lassoed" expertly with a long leash by one of the attendants; and a good thing this was too, for she might easily have been killed in that heavily-trafficked street that hot summer afternoon.

The Civic Arena at the Shelter was big and cavernous, with lots of room for the outsize cages for the big dogs, and plenty of space left for any of us to roam around in and walk dogs, on a rainy day. Often I used to talk and sing to the dogs when we couldn't go outdoors — simple songs, where no one could hear me. They all liked music. "My Old Kentucky Home" and "Home On The Range" were two of their favorites. They liked "Onward Christian Soldiers," too, because I put action into it, as I marched up and down in front of their cages like a soldier. The Shelter dogs were never exactly spellbound with my singing, however, like Glindy and Ceridwen had been, and soon there was so much competition from *their* voices, I had to let them take over the solo work.

Humphrey (named after Senator Hubert Humphrey) was a big dog. A male, abandoned and brought to the Shelter by the Police with a terrible case of mange, Humphrey was as sweet a dog as you'll ever want to know, even with his agonizing affliction. One day passing his cage and seeing his two front legs, blood-red and inflamed with the mange, I said, "Oh, what's the matter with my poor boy?" and he actually lifted up his front legs — one at a time — to *show* me what was the matter.

Not many corgis, or corgi-mixes, came to the Shelter for adoption, but I remember two, though they weren't there long enough for us to get acquainted. I was lucky, however, to be present when one was adopted, having just met him and taken him for a walk. We had had a chummy time during the walk and I told him about Glindy and Cerid. When we got back from the walk, the young couple who had surreptitiously been watching us before making their decision, finally chose *him* for adoption and allowed me to say good-bye to him. So I held his face in my hands and told him about being a good boy now that he was going to a new home. That dog never took his eyes from me and it was as though we had known each other always and fully understood one another. This greatly impressed his new owners, though I never even got to know the dog's name, nor *their* names, adoptions being a confidential matter at the Shelter.

A big, jolly old St. Bernard dog in the Civic Arena section of the Shelter, greeted me amiably every Tuesday. Because of his size and appetite he was a long time being adopted, as big dogs usually are. So all of us Volunteers got to know him well. Sammy, his name was, and he lumbered along day by day in his extra-large cage, just like an overweight human being. He reminded me of Santa Claus a little and I felt if we could have put a Santa Claus suit on him and stood him up on his hind legs, he could easily have passed for Old St. Nick himself, at Christmas time. Or better still, if we could have seated him behind a glass-topped desk, he might have been a dead-ringer for Winston Churchill. At last the day came for Sammy to be adopted, and go to a good home in the country. It was only then I learned that Sammy was a "she," and had the prim, ladylike name of Samantha — "Sammy" for short. So we all had a good laugh about that!

There were countless other precious dogs and precious experiences at the Shelter. There was the dog that every time I took him for a walk stood on his hind legs to look in every car for his master, never dreaming his master had purposely *lost* him. Then there was the dog that ran up the steps of every front door that had them, expecting to be let in, from force of habit. . . . There was also the beautiful Siamese cat, who when I opened her cage door to stroke her, immediately leaped out and draped herself around my neck, also from force of habit, that being the affectionate way she had greeted her former mistress. . . . And there was the unforgettable dachsund, who despite his diminutive size, walked straight and tall like a General. He was a joy to see on our one and only outing together, for he had already been adopted before my next Tuesday at the Shelter . . . and there were the friendly cats and kittens that playfully stuck their paws out through their cage bars to give me a little poke on the head as a reminder that *they* were there too, when I paid too much attention to the puppies.

I might say here, before another word, the Shelter people know nothing about these observations, or the fact that I'm writing them, so they are exclusively *my own* impressions. But one impression I had above all others was that the dogs were acutely aware, most of them, of *why* they were at the Shelter, and of the intentions of the countless visitors passing by and peering into their cages. They all seemed to have a sixth sense about this, and some of them actually turned their backs and walked away from certain visitors, while pleading for attention from others.

There was one German shepherd dog I remember who passionately wanted to be adopted by a certain young man and his family that stood before his cage. He was patient and on his best behavior about it for a long time, while they took forever to make up their minds. Their choice had been narrowed to a handsome Irish setter or the eager German shepherd, both dogs guaranteed to be fond of children.

At last the decision was made for the German shepherd. When the attendant opened the door to let him out, he made one great leap of joy for the father of the family, his new master, licking him all over; then dutifully hugged the mother and children, individually. Everyone was laughing at the dog's actions and by the time the adoption papers were signed that German shepherd was so overjoyed he was kissing everybody in the Shelter, not only his new family, but all the rest of us. It was one adoption we felt good about, down deep inside.

I could go on and on with stories about the cats and dogs at the Shelter, but this is Ceridwen's story, and we must get on with it. So I'll tell you about the Christmas Party that year at the Shelter, and then return to Ceridwen.

* * * * *

Chapter 12

THE PARTY

The invitation said it was "a Christmas Party for the Dogs — to be given by the Volunteers" that first year I became one, and this meant instead of beings guests, as usual, we were hosts, along with the Board Members and certain invited friends of the Shelter. The date was a Sunday, two weeks before Christmas; the time: from five to eight, a new party-time for me, but I saw the minute I got there, *this* party really was "for the dogs," and they knew it. Late, because of a previous commitment, it was going strong by the time I arrived, and it was hilarious!

All the dogs had been let out of their cages and were assembled in the "Civic Arena section" as I called it, and it was filled to overflowing. The Volunteers were walking the dogs and it was hard to say who was having the best time, guests or hosts, for they were all equally joyful and had just finished a game of "Musical Chairs" I was sorry to have missed, for it would have been fun to see dogs and people in a competition of this kind. Outside, the weather was horrendous, with a howling wind and sleety rain, but inside, the weather was all sunshine.

The dogs had been "partnered" indiscriminately, so as not to hurt any-one's feelings, and this led to an assortment and momentum hard to describe in words, but the end-effect was infinitely gay, like a party with too much inebriation. But here, and I give you my word, nothing stronger than pop and lemonade had touched the lips of either dog or man, proving you can get just as "high" on lemonade as strong drink, if you want to. Of course some lucky souls had devoured the doughnuts and coffee before I got there, and we Volunteers were destined to wait for a covered-dish dinner later in the evening, after the dogs had been put to bed. Plainly, and for everybody to see, some of the "guests" had already retired, and were looking out dis-consolately from their cages at their hosts, the "night on the town" having been too much for them, and the ways of mankind beyond understanding.

I cast a wary eye over the assembly looking for my two special friends, Nicky and Taffy, but didn't have to look long, because Taffy spotted me first and the little imp almost knocked me down with her welcome. Nicky, I learned, had been adopted two or three days earlier, and was thus absent. Accompanied by an attractive young lady, Taffy was obviously enjoying herself and didn't need me around, so I wended my way to the Puppy

81

Room. Wonder of wonders, there was pandemonium there, too, with the puppies all out of their cages, and running around gleefully with teen-agers and youngsters after them.

The cats, more shy and cautious, were roosting outside the tops of their cages, or draped about the shoulders or necks of young lads, who were evidently children of the Volunteers. More wonders. They (the cats) weren't arching their backs up at the puppies, either, and seemed to be taking the whole scene for granted, with true Christmas spirit, although some of them had chosen to remain in their opened cages for the duration, for safety's sake. They were looking out defensively at the rest of us. This really was a party for everybody, cats, dogs, kids, puppies, kittens and people alike. It was wonderful!

Taffy's admirer by this time had come to find me and turn her little charge over to me. So I walked my weekly friend around the Arena two or three times, greeting everyone along the way, after which Taffy and I retired to a corner for a little Christmas peace and quiet, but she was of another mind. So I decided to give my Christmas present to her then and there. Nicky's present, I had left at the door with Santa Claus.

She sized up the present, licked it all over, and then settled down to devouring it, which was all right, because it was one of those beef-flavored toys that I felt like sampling myself. She was going at it lustily and speedily, when an itinerant photographer roamed by and yelled, "hold it," obviously to me and took Taffy's picture, which ought to make the Shelter's "Hall of Fame," if not the Hollywood circuit.

It was a fabulous party by any standard, with everyone glad to be there without exception; and if anyone tells you dogs and cats don't know how to behave at parties, you can certainly set them straight on that score.

Chapter 13

MEMORIES ARE FOREVER: GLAD OR SAD

Our Cup of Tea Had A History...

Once upon a time, long ago — when Cerid wasn't even born yet and Glindy was a six-months-old puppy newly arrived from Wales, in the town of Ambridge, Pennsylvania, where our mill was located — I was walking through the mill one day looking for stories for the mill magazine, when one of the men stopped me and asked: "How goes it with the new puppy?" He was the soul of sympathy as I told him everything, never showing the ghost of a smile until I mentioned the fact that Glindy and I had a cup of tea together every day, when I went home for lunch, and to walk him.

"Did you say 'a cup of tea'?" he asked, trying not to laugh.

"Of course," I answered, "What's wrong with *that*?"

Then he laughed and thumped his thighs so hard I thought he would have a stroke.

By this time the other men in the department wanted in on the joke, so they gathered around from the various machines and workbenches nearby, while he told them about "the cup of tea." They, too, split their sides laughing, so there was nothing for me to do but laugh with them, although for the life of me I couldn't see that a cup of tea was all *that* funny. So, shrugging my shoulders, I left them to continue on my way looking for stories. I noticed, however, that the incident, somehow miraculously, had lifted my sagging spirits, and stuck in my mind as a pleasant memory.

After I retired and was living in Pittsburgh, Glindy, Cerid and I always knew lunchtime meant "a cup of tea," though neither of them had ever tasted the beverage in their lives. I'd say, "Let's get our cup of tea," and they were always ready. The British would have called it neither a "high tea," nor a "low tea," and if the men in the mill had been present, they would surely have called it a dull one, but it filled the bill for us, and was a high-spot in our daily living.

When Glindy died, Cerid and I kept up the custom, though often it was a mixed pleasure when she contracted diabetes, and food became an eternal problem. For her, the "cup of tea" was perhaps just a leftover tidbit from the previous night's supper, a thin slice of cheese, or perhaps only a cracker.

83

But it became a sweet-time for both of us, despite everything, and now she's no longer living, a treasured memory.

The "Cup Of Tea" must have made a lasting impression on the mill men involved in it, too, because long after I retired and was visiting in Ambridge one day, someone told me that one of those men was ill, and in fact dying. So I called at his home to see him, and the *first* thing he said was: "Tell me about the cup-of-tea," which I did, and both of us had a good laugh together, all over again. *He* definitely hadn't forgotten the incident. So, you see, our little repast had a "history," and even the famous Boston Tea Party couldn't boast more than that!

* * * * *

Cerid and the Weather

Whatever the weather may be, may be
Whatever the weather may be. . .
It's the songs you sing, and the smiles you wear
That make the sunshine everywhere
And the world a place of glee.
— Source Unknown

Oh the days are here that Ceridwen loved, were *she* only here to enjoy them! For she revelled in Autumn weather!

Spring, summer, winter, she enjoyed them all except summer, when she could hardly breathe. But come autumn, with its cool air, crackling leaves and trees well-laden with apples, and she was happy to be alive, eating them.

Spring meant noisy, playful schoolchildren going up and down 40th Street, whom we watched from our hideout in the Sanctuary. Spring, also, meant muddy streets, which she hated.

Winter was fun when she was young and could romp in the snow. But as she grew older its discomforts plainly plagued her, and nothing could induce her to remain long outdoors.

* * * * *

The Stick!

These next few paragraphs are not for disciplinarians, so please skip them if you're one. They pertain to Obedience, a worthy trait, but never one of Cerid's strong points; and sometimes she would persist in so many acts of mischief, and disobey so many rules there was nothing for the situation but The Stick!

I'd say, "If you don't watch, I'll get The Stick," — first as warning, but there was no response, because she could see I hadn't budged. Then realizing this was getting us nowhere fast, I'd stomp over to the magazine rack where the harmless little tree branch we had so glorified lay quietly at rest; and the effect was electric! She'd jump to attention, ready for obedience or anything.

Capitalizing on the effect, in time the little tree branch became a marvellous symbol of authority.

In reality, the poor quivering little tree branch couldn't have smacked down a flea or a fly if both had stood still and waited for the blows. But somehow, and the Lord be praised, it became a deadly weapon to Cerid. Once it was raised aloft over her head, the battle for me was won. Luckily she never did catch on to what a puny blow it would have delivered, and this was a good thing for both of us.

In all fairness to her, however, when Obedience really *did* matter, she was its very soul, for she knew by my voice that it *was* or *wasn't* important, and if it *was*, she gave it her utmost attention.

* * * * *

"Whatcha Got?"

"Whatcha Got" was a happy little game Cerid and I sometimes played in the house, and it could be played anytime she was in a playful mood. She usually requested the game herself by bringing something to me in her mouth, and I would say, all interested: "What do you have in your mouth?" which, for brevity's sake, became: "Whatcha Got?"

It sounds like an overly childish pastime but it gave her pleasure and anything that buoyed her spirits during diabetic days was a godsend and I was all for it. Sometimes the article which she held tightly between her teeth would be a bobby pin she had found on the floor, and it was the devil's own job to extricate from her teeth. Another time the center of interest might be an earring, which, too, was fiendish to "retrieve." One weird object she carried home one time was a rubber spark plug.

The game presented countless variations because anything I would drop and she could pick up was fair game and it was unbelievable how many droppable things a small efficiency apartment *could* hold, all of them dangerous to her, from my point of view. But it was good to see her laughing and enjoying the sport.

Occasionally I'd get the shivers and think "Oh it might be a needle or a pin, or a thimble—what next?" and remember the time Glindy swallowed the sock when we were living in Sewickly, and were playing a tug-of-war game. Everyone was a wreck (even the vet) until he passed it, for it would have meant a major operation if he hadn't.

But luck was with Cerid and we never had a catastrophe with our "Whatcha Got" game. She'd stand in front of me with a happy look, usually when my hands were in the dishwater, or occupied with a bagful of groceries. No matter! Her eyes shining with merriment, she'd allow me to *look* at the object, not possess it, until I finally succeeded in retrieving it and then she, all tuckered-out, would retire to her corner for a rest.

"Whatcha Got?" therefore stands out poignantly in our book of memories, as Cerid's Game, because luckily Glindy favored larger objects to chase, which for me were easier to "retrieve."

* * * * *

Say "Cheese" and say it softly . . .

In fact you might almost whisper it.

After Cerid got diabetes and was on a rigid formula diet, a rare deviation from the diet was a slice of packaged cheese, or some other little food snack —which she waited and watched for patiently every time the refrigerator door was opened. In fact so longingly, that doling it out almost became a ritual—a sort of sacrament, as it were.

In order to make the slice last longer, for she would have swallowed it whole, I had to cut it in pieces so small there could hardly have been much taste to them; but she grabbed them so fast I had to be quick about it, or else stand the chance of losing the tip of my finger, because she was so excited about getting each tidbit.

* * * * *

Afraid of Storms

When she was very young and first came to America, Cerid was terrified of storms, and would hide under the bed at the first sign of thunder and lightning, staying there as long as the storm lasted and only coming out once in a while for a breath of air. I always knew beforehand that a storm was coming by her antics, for she would stop whatever she was doing and follow me everywhere around the apartment.

Glindy would sit unperturbed, watching her momentarily.

I would say: "The storm won't hurt you . . . look, it *can't* get in when I pull the blind down," and suddenly yank it almost to the windowsill. Glindy, by this time, was nuzzling up to her and saying soothing things in her ear, when bang, there was a new clap of thunder and vivid flash of lightning, and under the bed she would go again—this last one that lit up the whole apartment even with the blinds down—and Glindy, too, would retire to the safety zone under the bed.

Finally *all* the electric lights would go out and we were in total darkness indoors and outdoors. This lasted several minutes, until the storm abated, it stopped raining, and the lights came on as Glindy and Cerid ran to the front door waiting to be let out for their "exercises." I looked out the window at them and they were rolling around in the wet grass with abandon, getting a quick bath. *That* part of the storm they both liked. So they stayed outdoors playing until they were dry and sparkling clean.

* * * * *

Speaking of Baths (The Formal Kind, With Soap and Water)

Giving Cerid a "real" bath, *indoors*, was something else again, almost an "occasion" you could call it. There was no special day for the event; it was just any day she seemed to be needing it, except in wintertime when there was likelihood of catching cold.

Glindy was always first to get in and out of the bathtub, which helped matters because she would do anything he did, and when she saw him splashing around in the water merrily, she was more or less ready, when *her* turn came, though none too enthusiastic. This entailed two baths instead of one and a thoroughly unnecessary one often for Glindy, but he was willing to accept the ordeal for Cerid's sake.

She stalled as long as possible hoping I would change my mind. When there had been enough stalling I would summon her sharply and then began the chase around the living room to corner her into the bathroom with a newspaper. Giving a look at Glindy to see if he would save her and finding him of no help, she *allowed* herself to be eased into the warm water. Holding her down with one hand and rubbing shampoo into their coats with the other, usually resulted in a bath for the three of us. Actually she was so afraid of being "trapped" in the tub I had to "shower" her with compliments during the whole ordeal, to make her forget her plight.

But after it was all over, she was plainly pleased with herself and wanted Glindy to admire her. Which he did, nosing her all over, thus putting the finishing touches to the drying process, fortunately.

* * * * *

"The Magic Carpet"

It was just a wee piece of carpet in front of a numbered door at the end of a long, confusing hall, as Cerid hurried to it after coming in from a walk. She'd hurry as fast as her short legs and aging body would carry her, and stand there triumphantly — with a grin or a grunt, depending on how she felt for the day. Pleased when she made it — and proud — that this was *her* door, her home, her refuge — in the unnatural apartment-life we were living.

Sometimes when she was tired she mistakenly stopped at a nearer door; other times when she was feeling playful she did this for fun and to tease me, laughing mischievously when I said, "No! *that's* not our door and you know it."

She was always first in our procession down the hall, as though she couldn't wait to get to her own little domain. Once inside, familiar things reassured her as she settled down contentedly to enjoy her home and castle.

That little piece of carpet was for her like the famous flying carpet in the Arabian Nights, and I have kept it at our door in her memory.

* * * * *

One Christmas Eve

In our world of holdups and rampage on the city streets, walking at night was out of the question for most people. Yet Cerid and I always took our nightly walk without fail, and looked forward to it — never fearing holdups or danger of any kind. Everybody was in bed in our apartment-building; all was still, and we were monarchs of all we surveyed for those brief and memorable midnight moments. Naturally we didn't stray far from our block-long-building precincts and we didn't flaunt ourselves or invite adventure in any way. Once in a while a questionable-looking passerby did pass us, muttering things we couldn't hear and therefore didn't have to heed. Otherwise our serenity was unbroken.

Always a serene being, night implemented Cerid's serenity, and bolstered her composure. No one said, "Hi, Cerid," to interrupt hers and my thoughts, and the night-walk became the chummiest outing of our day. Glindy was alive when we first came to the apartment and he too had loved the night-walk. After he went to Heaven Cerid and I felt his presence most keenly *at night.*

Apartment friends cautioned us so much about our night-walks we sometimes felt we were disturbing them, but they always said "No." There were the stars to light our way and the ever-present floodlights surrounding our apartment building. So we felt safe at all times. Buses went eerily by outside the gate, sparsely filled with late home-goers, and though we could see them through our hedges — in the semiconsciousness of our dreamworld — they never intruded or bothered us.

One Christmas Eve at midnight we watched the flickering lights of the U. S. Steel Building in downtown Pittsburgh faraway. The narrow perpendicular windows gave out a subdued, candle-like glow unlike the dazzling lights of the other buildings. Turning to Cerid, I asked: "How many windows would you say there are in the U. S. Steel Building, hundreds? thousands? just give a guess. . . ."

But she paid no attention to my question, as we stood silently a long while savoring the night's peace and watching the whole world slowly merge into the intimacy and holiness of Christmas Eve.

Softly, and not to break the spell, I hummed, "Silent Night, Holy Night" as Cerid raptly listened. Feeling almost shy in the awesomeness of the moment, I said, "Merry Christmas, Cerid — the angels are singing . . . can you *hear* them?"

Yes, she could hear them, for with ears standing up like antennas, she was listening for all she was worth to their voices, that Christmas Eve in the year of our Lord 1975.

* * * * *

PART THREE

Chapter 14

LETTERS TO AND ABOUT CERIDWEN

"A Packet of Pills"

Approximately two months after Ceridwen died, I asked the girls at the Veterinary Hospital, where she had spent so much time after getting diabetes — whether they had any special memories of her they would like to share with me, explaining I hoped to write a book about her, as I had about Glindy. Here are two of the replies:

The first comes from *Wendy,* and it is about a packet of pills. "Yes," said Wendy, "I *do* have a memory that lingers, and it still makes me chuckle every time I think of it, though I'll never see friendly little Ceridwen again....

"You and I were talking one day while waiting for her to be discharged. She was sitting at your feet. I was holding some papers and a small packet of pills. The packet dropped quietly to the floor. Cerid immediately pounced on it and picked it up, holding it tightly between her teeth. I bent down to wrest it from her carefully, not wanting to spill any of the pills. But she just looked up at me sweetly and held tightly onto those pills. I tried every wile at my command, but stubborn little dear that she was, she just *wouldn't* let go of that packet of pills. So you and I continued our conversation, until her mouth got so tired of holding onto it she accidentally dropped the packet on the floor.

"Then it was *my* turn to pounce. So I grabbed those pills faster than fast, and hid them behind me, out of her reach. Was she ever surprised! The look on her face was comical. I'll never forget it and that sweet little memory nor her delight, in holding onto those pills.

"I know you must miss her terribly, and I am glad you are sharing your time and love for animals with the dogs at the Animal Shelter. God bless you and little Cerid . . . we miss her here at the hospital. . . ."

— Wendy

* * * * *

Shirley, at the Veterinary Hospital, sent us Albert Schweitzer's *"Prayer For Animals"* as *her* "Memory" of Cerid. She had diligently reproduced it, art work and all, on parchment-like paper, from an original copy of the

Prayer she had seen somewhere. It is a beautiful piece of work I have kept to this day, and I am grateful to both Wendy and Shirley for their "Memories."

A Prayer For Animals

Hear our humble prayer, O God, for our friends the animals,
    Especially for animals who are suffering;
      For any that are hunted, or lost, or deserted, or frightened, or hungry.
      For *all* that must be put to death.
We entreat for them *all,* Thy mercy and pity;
      And for those who deal with them, we ask a heart of compassion,
And gentle hands, and kindly words.
      Make us ourselves to be true friends to animals, and
So to share the blessings of the merciful.

                                     — Albert Schweitzer

* * * * *

"All the Way . . ."

The following poem was sent to us by *Phoebe Davis,* a Welsh friend and former Pittsburgher now living in Florida. She sent it as a consolation-piece when Cerid died, and it had been written by the son of her neighbor across the street when he was a young man living in California. Many years later the son was found dead of a heart attack, his little half-dead dog beside him. The dog had been watching over his master's body for four days when the body was found, and died immediately after. So *that* "little old dog" did follow his master right "to the cross," and everyone wondered how the young man knew this would happen so many years *before* it did.

My Dog

I wonder if Christ had a little dog,
 All silky and shiny like mine?
With a nose always wet, two beautiful ears,
 And two brown eyes tender, that shine. . .

I'm sure if He had, that *that* little dog
 Knew right from the start He was God;
And he needed no proof that Christ was divine
 And just worshipped the ground where He trod.

I'm afraid Christ didn't, because I have read
 How He prayed in the garden alone
When all His friends and disciples had fled,
 Even Peter, the one that they stoned.

So I feel pretty sure Christ had no dog,
 And *that,* I guess, was *His* loss,
Because if He had a dog loyal as mine,
 It would have followed Him right to the Cross.

* * * * *

Letters To Ceridwen

For a long time *after* she died I felt so close to Ceridwen it was as though she was still alive and standing beside me. Then I would talk to her, out loud, as we had talked together during her lifetime, being careful to do so when no one was around to think me crazy. To be talked to was what she liked, and it was a way of bringing us together. I wish now in retrospect I had jotted down more of the talking-out-loud incidents, as they came and went, but here are two, at least, by way of illustration. They are in letter form.

Dear Ceridwen,

Something has just happened that I must tell you about, even if you *are* in Heaven, and will you please let Glindy know about this because he'll be interested, too? Remember how afraid you, Glindy and I used to be of German shepherd dogs, he not so afraid as you and I, but still cautious because they were forever challenging him?

Well, this morning I went downstairs to pick up a parcel post item the apartment office had telephoned me about. Digging around in the large collection of parcels for one with my name on, my back was turned to everything and everybody, and I had not seen or heard anyone entering the office.

Suddenly rising from my stooped position to tell the office secretary I couldn't find the package, I looked straight into the eyes of a big, brown German shepherd dog, right there in our apartment office! It was an incredible sight and for a moment I thought: "*This* isn't Tuesday, my day at the Animal Shelter."

The dog stood looking at me, and without the slightest fear, I asked him: "What are *you* doing here?" and seeing him friendly, gave him a pat on the back. He didn't resent the overture, so I continued patting him and saying, "Good boy, good boy."

Then I saw the halter!

Recognizing it for a "Seeing Eye" dog contrivance, I lifted my eyes higher and looked into the pleasant face of a blind girl, his mistress. This all happened in a matter of minutes, and feeling confident I looked around and saw *another* blind girl, with a *coal-black* German shepherd dog. Thinking that dog might be feeling hurt because I hadn't patted *him,* too, I gave him a friendly pat, noticing all the while that his tail was thumping the floor happily, just like the brown dog's tail.

The office secretary was speechless during this little drama and there wasn't a word from either of the blind girls — so suddenly realizing I had broken a cardinal rule of the Seeing Eye dog training program that no one but the owner is supposed to touch or talk to a Seeing Eye dog, I stammered, "Oh, excuse me" and scooted out of the office *fast!*

Cerid, this was an unbelievable experience and perhaps you will want to give *me* a pat on the back for being so brave, but the truth is I don't deserve it for I didn't feel the slightest fear with those two dogs. So it couldn't have been bravery. But it *does* go to show that German shepherd dogs *can* be friendly, and I'm glad, and won't be so afraid of them in the future.

(A postscript to this letter is I never DID find out what those dogs and their blind owners, were doing in our apartment office, which is just as well, for it was none of my business anyway.)

* * * * *

New Year's Eve Letter to Ceridwen, 1977

Dear Cerid:

You have gone from this earth almost ten months. I still miss you, and am here in our Sanctuary, to spend a holiday moment with you; and only a moment, because there is a cruel, wintry dampness in the air, and it's getting chillier by the minute.

Each night this past week I have been watching in vain for the downtown Christmas lights to go on, but there is an energy shortage these days in America, and President Carter has asked everyone to "conserve." Thus, many downtown buildings have not been "lighting up" as usual for this year's Holiday Season. Remember the lovely Christmas lights we watched together — you, Glindy and I, when we were all here on *this* earth? I do!

It is now the Sunset Hour. We loved the sunset hour, we three.

The great ball of fire, orange-red at this moment, is slowly sinking into the horizon — going. . .going. . .*Gone* — for its night of rest and seclusion. How quickly it vanished from sight!

It has been a beautiful day, a jewel of a day, irrelevantly set in the bleakness of winter to give peace to our souls and strength, during another annual orgy of Christmas buying and giving.

You are silently, as in a dream, running up and down the high cyclone fence behind the Infirmary — barking at the trucks and people passing by. Yet there isn't a sound, for this is a *spiritual* rendezvous we are having, and you and I are here to commemorate our past years together; to ask God's blessing for the New Year, that is to come. *Happy New Year to you, Ceridwen, in Heaven; and to Glindy, too, in this year of our Lord, 1977.*

ABOVE: We thought you'd like to see this long-ago picture (at age two months) of the four members of Cerid's first litter before you look at their "today" (1979) picture. All of them are still living except little Honey (AKC name, Glyncerid Simplicity). She's the one on the extreme left, and she died several years ago during her first childbirth. The other three are Glyncerid Felicity and Audacity; and Osage Midget.

TOBY

TWM

MIDGE GANU

FOUR GOOD REASONS FOR REJOICING

Toby, Midgie and Ganu are the three surviving members of Ceridwen's first family, sired by Champion Ehrstag's Farleu.

Twm Shon Catti is the sole surviving member of Glindy's and Ceridwen's big family. You read all about their untimely deaths in the chapter on Motherhood.

Toby — and this isn't a dramatic pose he's affecting. He's merely waiting for the flashbulb to go off — then he'll run to cover and hide until the camera is safely out of sight.　　　　(picture credit—*Averill Jones*)

Twm Shon Catti (Twm) — and not a good picture of the jolly "Twm", which we can say because we took it. Twm, like Toby, is averse to picture-taking, but he reacts by walking away from the camera *before* the shutter clicks and the flashbulb goes off. Toby does wait until *after*.

Midgie — likes nothing better than to lie at her master's side when he sits in his favorite chair writing sermons.　　(picture credit—*John Frame*)

Ganu's— regal posture herein comes natural to her. Her home is her Castle and her family her Kingdom, and she takes her duties seriously in her large home, with a family of four and two mischievous dogs to look after.　　　　　　　　(picture credit—*Susan Smith*)

— *The stories of all four dogs have been delightfully told by their doting masters in this chapter.*

Chapter 15

"BLEST BE THE TIE THAT BINDS
AND REJOICES OUR HEARTS FOREVER"
IT'S CERIDWEN

In the chapter about Ceridwen's Motherhood we told you mostly about the puppies of her *second* litter and what happened to *them* — this being the litter that *Glindy* sired and the hoped-for litter of my life. Now comes the story of what happened to the offspring of Ceridwen's *first* litter, sired by Champion Ehrstag's *Farleu* and it has a happier ending as you shall see.

Nearly twelve years old at this writing, three of that first litter still survive and are all well and happy. Corgis usually do not live inordinately long lives, and the longevity of these three attests to the loving care and good homelife they have enjoyed through the years. "Honey," the fourth of the Farleu off-spring, was first sold to a Welsh-born couple from Pembrokeshire but had been resold by them to a friend who wanted to breed her. Sad to say, she died in her first childbirth.

"Honey," "Precious," "Jumbo" and "Mickey Mouse," to whom I had also given facetious names in the whelping box, became "Felicity," "Simplicity," "Audacity" and "Osage Midget" when they were registered with the American Kennel Club and received their *official* names.

Starting with "Osage Midget" — the first to leave the fold when Mr. Clark Frame came to claim her as his "pick-of-the-litter" stud fee — went to his home in the Virginia Manor section of Pittsburgh. Later his son John took her to live with him, near Philadelphia. John Frame is a man with many degrees in philosophy and religion from Princeton, Yale and Westminster Seminary. In 1968 he was ordained a minister of the Orthodox Presbyterian Church, and also taught at Westminster Seminary, both in Philadelphia. Presently he is pastor, organist and choir director at Community Orthodox Presbyterian Church in Blue Bell, Pennsylvania. An extremely busy young man, "Midgie" as he calls her, keeps his home fires burning brightly, and is his devoted helpmate at all times. This is what he has to say about her:

"When Midgie (Osage Midget) first came to our family home in Pittsburgh as a puppy, she was in a Cinderella situation. Although she got along fine with her father 'Farleu,' she had a hard time with the other two female dogs in the house, her 'wicked stepmother' and 'wicked stepsister,' who were

99

jealous of her. Mother and Dad then decided she'd be happier somewhere else, and I became 'Prince Charming.'

"She has been living with me since 1969 in the Philadelphia area of Pennsylvania, and has been a great delight. Since I am a bachelor, she is my home and family. I have spoiled her, but it's hard to avoid that.

"She's a big dog for a corgi, and somewhat overweight, due to lack of exercise, has never been frivolous, never enjoyed playing with a ball or a toy, or taking long walks. But she *can* be energetic when something *really* important is going on, like when a rabbit strays into our yard, or a knock comes to the door.

"I get my mail through a slot in the door, and Midgie lies in wait for the mailman. Then she grabs the mail between her teeth as it comes through the slot, barking ferociously.

"She also gets very excited about animals on TV, and even in still pictures. I had had the impression that animals were incapable of recognizing shapes in two dimensions, and without the aid of smell. However, I taught Midgie the meaning of 'dog' and 'cat,' up to a point; and one day when I pointed out a dog on TV, a flash of recognition came over her. Now she barks at *any* animal on TV, but not at humans, unless they have lots of hair, fur coats, etc.; or are making odd noises.

"She is an awfully good girl. I don't need a leash with her in most situations, and she is the only corgi I know, about which *that* can be said. She is very loyal, asks my permission if anyone wants to pet her, or take her for a walk, and is the best house-trained dog I've *ever* known.

'Despite her weight problem, I think she's a *real* beauty, for she has one of the prettiest faces I've ever seen, set off by enormous black, concerned, serious eyes. I love her dearly, and hope she can spend many more years with me."

— John Frame

* * * * *

Ganu

Little "Precious" (AKC name "Felicity") was the next to leave home and went to Mr. and Mrs. James Smith, at that time living in Atlanta, Georgia, where Jim Smith, the husband, was a practicing lawyer. The Smiths had two children, Karen (now age fifteen) and David (now thirteen), but it took their Welsh grandmother, Mrs. Mae Hoffman, of Washington, D.C., to give the puppy her lasting name: "Ganu," pronounced Ganee, with a hard "g". Seeing the new little member of the family, Mae Hoffman was delighted and said "Oh, she's like a song—let's call her 'Ganu'" (the Welsh verb for singing). The name stuck. Ganu lives a busy life nowadays in her latest home in Charlotte, North Carolina. Sue Smith, the young mother of the Smith family, tells the Ganu story:

"Ganu arrived at the Smith household on a flight from Pittsburgh when she was not quite three months old. The two children and I spent several nervous hours at Atlanta airport waiting for a plane with a pressurized baggage compartment, needed for transporting her. When her crate *did* appear, there was a sad and bewildered little puppy peering out at the world. We took her home, stayed up all night with her, and were pleased when she adjusted quickly to her new surroundings.

Within a year we moved to Philadelphia, where she spent seven years enjoying a lovely suburban yard. While there, she had to adjust to the arrival of first—a cat (many hours were spent chasing the cat around the house, nipping at its heels)—and later two puppies, one part beagle and the other mostly 'mutt'. How different they were from our corgi!

"Ganu has several well-developed personality traits. Her 'herding' instinct, for instance, for which corgis are famous the world over, is quite strong. She is also a wonderful watchdog, always alert for a strange noise, and we really appreciate this trait. She barks when it is time for the children to go to school, when it's time to fix dinner; and when it's time to go to bed. She tries her *best* to teach the other two dogs manners, barking at them when they misbehave.

"She is well-travelled, having spent a month near Quebec City, Canada, managing to get around in three feet of snow, and enjoys trips to the beach, where although she avoids the water, she delights in chasing sand crabs. At an Atlantic City Dog Show to which we once took her, she distinguished herself by winning a blue ribbon. Her favorite trip, however, is to Washington, D.C., where my mother lives and adores her, though she tries hard not to spoil her.

"We are now living in the center of Charlotte, North Carolina, and Ganu is learning to become a city dweller, surrounded by the sights and sounds of a bulldozer as construction work is being done on our lovely old Victorian neighborhood. But she sometimes likes to get away from it all by going with us to our cottage in the North Carolina mountains. There she has freedom to run at will and express her love for mountain scenery, a lurking love that's in *every* Welshman.

"Ganu loves us *all* with equal devotion, and we love her; in fact it's hard sometimes to say who loves whom best. . . ."

— Susan Smith

* * * * *

Toby

Toby ("Audacity," his AKC name) the largest of the litter when he was born and the adorable little boss of them all, like Ganu, was sold through our ad in the Welsh-American newspaper; but went farthest away, to northern Minnesota, where Mr. and Mrs. W. K. Jones, his new owners, were in the educational field—"Ken" Jones being principal of the school in his area. Though now retired, the Joneses are still in the educational field, and these past two years (1977-1979), along with a dozen other dedicated educational people from all over the United States, are volunteer teachers at a large school for disadvantaged black children in the deep South (Mississippi).

Averill Jones, Toby's mistress, works in the Elemental Library and also tutors four children in reading and arithmetic. She plays for the church services on Sunday mornings, while "Ken" Jones, her husband has been working in an advisory capacity, as well as serving as a counselor to the youngsters. Toby fitted right into their school life and has been as much "at home" in Mississippi as Minnesota. Averill here gives the report on his daily activities:

"Like a clock—everything for Toby has to be done on schedule. Mornings I open the door of the closet where he sleeps and he stands up to have his tummy rubbed with words of endearment. Then Ken washes his face with a Kleenex tissue, after which he has breakfast and goes out for his first airing.

"When we first arrived at the school he barked at the boys (frightening them), and we scolded him. Now they don't pay any attention to him, nor he to them. He has a large beautiful park to roam in. When we are at school during the day, he sleeps. At noon we come home for lunch and a brief walk with him. *After* school we take him for a long walk and come home to rest on our lovely screened porch where he watches everything that goes on. He is an excellent companion, barks when the telephone or doorbell rings and comes to get us to answer them. If Ken is in the next room, instead of calling him I tell Toby to go get him and he understands perfectly.

"A 'seasoned' traveller, he has no complaints in the car or on the road and has spent three winters in California. Curling up in the back seat, he's contented to stay there night or day, and is a good watchdog on our trips.

"About the 'closet' I mentioned earlier, all he asks at night is a warm, comfortable closet to sleep in. Our friends think this strange, and it worried *us* for a long time, too, but we don't fret about it any more, because that is what he *definitely* wants. He's a very human little fellow and makes his wants known with short barks which we call 'talking to us.' My husband takes him for a second long walk daily—just the two of them—and he enjoys exploring everything along the way. We've never had any trouble disciplining him, but he is quite aware his mistress doesn't always mean No, when he coaxes for a tasty tidbit.

"Ken and I love him dearly and he definitely is 'a member of the family.'"

— Averill Jones

* * * * *

Twm

Now comes Twm—"Twm Shon Catti" his AKC name, but Twm is all he has ever been known by.

Named after the famous Welsh "Robin Hood" of long ago, he is the sole survivor of Glindy's and Cerid's lovely litter, described in Chapter Five of this, Ceridwen's story; and he ably represents his parents and his brothers and sisters herein. You learned in Chapter Five of the untimely or tragic deaths of the remainder of the litter, so we won't repeat these sad facts now, but will let Emily Istvan tell Twm's story. But before she begins, we might say Twm was born on June 6, 1970 and was bought by Mr. and Mrs. John Istvan of East McKeesport, Pennsylvania, a borough about fourteen miles from Pittsburgh when he was approximately four months old. John Istvan is a retired salesman for a large ice-cream company in Pittsburgh and Emily was born in a big house in East McKeesport a few feet away from her present abode, to which she came as a young bride. Her mother still lives in the old homestead. Here's Emily's story:

"We've always had dogs" says she, "and just before we got Twm we had an Irish setter, and he died. Setters and corgis are both gentle breeds and John and I have noticed they both have one outstanding character trait: responsibility. Give them something to do and they can be absolutely relied-upon to do it. Not all dogs are like that.

"The guarding instinct in Twm has always been strong and no one can come an inch nearer our house than he allows. In a sense, he guards my mother's house, too. If there is an unusual noise over there, he runs upstairs to our back bedroom window to investigate, giving a few warning barks to any caller or intruder. Then he runs downstairs to report on the situation to us.

"Even when we go for a ride, he stands up in the car as if he's taking care of everything, instead of lying down and enjoying himself as most dogs do. When we're getting gas at the filling station, Twm goes to the back seat and looks out the window at the attendant as though checking to see that he gives us the right amount of gasoline. When he's not busy that way he sits up front with us and thinks he's helping my husband to drive. He knows when the mailman is in the neighborhood, even in wintertime with our front door closed and when he's on the porch at mailtime he allows the mailman to deliver the mail, but not loiter, and barks as a gentle reminder. . . . He doesn't mind other dogs coming into our yard to play with him but lets them know whose yard it is, and he *loves* children. When our grandchildren come for a visit, he has the time of his life. They play 'Cops and Robbers' (Twm is the cop) and sometimes the game gets so realistic I have to go out and calm them all down, for fear they'll hurt themselves.

"The grandchildren take him for walks and one time they passed a small manufacturing concern near our house where the workers were on strike and the pickets said, 'Say, that little dog's feet and legs are getting shorter every time he passes here.' The children defended Twm and said it wasn't true, but when they got home they were in tears. So we all had a good laugh (Twm laughed too) when, after much explaining, they understood that the men were only teasing.

"He's not much for eating, but loves cabbage, and when I start to chop it up for salads or cooking, he's on hand in the kitchen waiting for a handout. And can he crunch cabbage! You can hear him all the way into the diningroom. It must be the 'crunch' that fascinates him. He doesn't like TV and will only come into the living room when there are dogs barking on the set, and he wants to have a look at them.

"People ask us if he's jealous, but the only time we've seen any evidence of it was when we first got him. My husband was still working then and Twm was used to being at home with me all day. He didn't like having a rival for my affections. So he chewed the cord of our electric blanket when we went to bed. Actually John made more fuss over him than I did, and soon he accepted us both with equal affection.

"He's an extremely affectionate little dog, and shows his affection in his expressive face, and loving ways. Sometimes we actually see him smile; and he loves to be out in the yard alone at night winter or summer. The night seems to hold a secret for him, and he comes indoors starry-eyed and refreshed. He always welcomes company, but enjoys being alone with us best. As soon as visitors leave he stretches out on his back, feet up in the air, as if to say 'let's take our shoes off and relax!' So we do.

"That's our Twm, and we love him!"

— Emily Istvan

In conclusion, and summing this all up, Ceridwen's mistress can do no better than to repeat what she has said in the heading of this chapter: "Blest Be the Tie That Binds . . . And Rejoices Our Hearts Forever."

The *tie*? It's Ceridwen, our own little Ceridwen, in whom, together with Midgie, Ganu, Toby, Twm, *and* their precious families and owners, we *do rejoice forever and forever. . . . Amen.*

* * * * *

Chapter 16

A FINAL LOOK AND FAREWELL

Ceridwen, for our last time together, and "farewell," (spiritually speaking, that is), let's go for a walk in our own neighborhood of Lawrenceville, and have a parting look at the old, familiar places we both knew and loved so well, when you were alive.

The "spiritual" parting with Glindy, remember? was in Wales, which he never really left in spirit, though living all but six months of his long life in America. But *your* spirit lingers here: in Arsenal Park by the swings where the children play; on our apartment grounds, where you rested so often and so contentedly; in the Sanctuary behind our grounds where you, Glindy and I went daily the months before he died. It was here you left and returned for visits to your beloved "Vet", and here, in Lawrenceville, your spirit lingers, and will, eternally.

It is a beautiful spring day, on the coolish side, exactly the sort of day you preferred to the lush days of summer. First, we will go down 39th Street, hoping once again, and for the last time, to decide *which* was the house where our old Welsh friend, Myfanwy King, lived long ago, before we moved to this neighborhood. Remember when we lived in Edgewood, and she came to visit us there? All tuckered out from her climb up Maple Avenue, we gave her a cup of tea to revive her, there being nothing better than a cup of tea to a Welshman. She came "to see the puppy," she said, you being then only five months old and but recently arrived from Wales. You and Glindy worked hard to entertain her, and I was proud of both of you.

Today we won't go down to the Allegheny River, as first planned, having been told its banks are too steep and slippery to descend. You look disappointed. Don't be! Everyone says there's not much to look at down there, anyway.

Wasn't it a surprise to find everything so alive and busy in Arsenal Park, this early in the year! All the recreational activties are in full swing, the tennis courts alive with players, the baseball field booming with baseballers . . . even the football field full of die-hard players, loath to let the football season go. Only the swings and slides were idle, it being naptime for the wee ones, and too early for their trip to the park.

Thirty-ninth Street looked the same as usual, Cerid, as we passed. The large complex of buildings belonging to Allegheny County Arsenal Health

Center, looked fresh and clean as always, and I imagine some of your old friends there might have been glad to see you, had they been looking out the window and feeling "spiritual," as *we* were. Everything was unchanged. . . .

However, just two streets away, on 37th Street, there was a *big* change, and I saw you sniffing the air as if to say, "That big building wasn't there when I went away." Explaining, I told you: "It's a new Senior Citizens' apartment house like ours, and it's already filled with tenants . . . its newness is a bit startling today, but never mind, the trees are beginning to sprout leaves, and trees will give it an old established look, eventually.

"While I think of it, Cerid, I saw your friend Susie the other day, the dog across the hall from our first apartment, remember her? She remembers you, and misses *you*, her walker told me. Do you miss her?

Coming up 40th Street and nearing home, our Sanctuary seemed bare and exposed-looking today. Strange, this, for we thought it quite cozy and intimate when you, Glindy and I went there daily. It was right, though, to call it "The Sanctuary," because those two huge stone enclosures for storage of rubbish, looked just like outdoor altars a minute ago when we passed them.

The street was noisy and busy with trucks and last stragglers of school-children as we reached the top of the hill, and we were glad to get inside our apartment gate, where everything was quiet. Cerid, your spiritual presence immediately quickened and became alive, when we got inside the gate. I *felt* you and started talking to you out loud, just as I used to. Chattering away, we circled the long, cement walk-around to the shuffleboard area fronting our apartment. Everything seemed as usual there, and it wasn't hard to imagine you at the window., teasing me as you used to. Just for the heck of it, I tapped on the window to attract your attention, but there was no Ceridwen to tap back. . . .

Now we have panted up the grassy slope to the high street fence, where you nosed along daily, enjoying the good things of the soil. Cerid, this is an embarrassing question and maybe you won't like it: "Did you ever dig up worms at that fence? I often wondered."

Oh! you're angry with the question, so I'll change the subject. Do you realize this *landscaping* wasn't even here when we moved to this apartment building, and Glindy didn't even *see* it before he died? He would have liked walking along this fence beside us, wouldn't he!

The breezes are getting balmy with the late afternoon sun and caress us as we move along. Notice this? You wanted to lie on the grass a minute ago, but I wouldn't let you with so much wintry dampness still left in the air.

See that little crab apple tree by our gate? Do you remember it was planted just before you went away? Well, it surely has made a brave effort to survive city life, and soon it will be covered with lovely rose-colored blossoms that by summertime will become tiny, scrawny, hard-as-rocks crab apples that even *you* wouldn't think of sampling!

Oh, Cerid, look at me now as we part. Always before, when we parted, for you to go to the vet, or some lesser reason, there was only a last long look between us, a reassuring smile, and my promise to "see you later," as I closed the door at the vet's hospital.

You have closed the door this time, to go to your Eternal Home. Go in peace, and with my profound blessing. Go to be with Glindy, and *wait* with him, till I come. The "promise" is, as always, to "see you later," and I will, Little One, and I *will*. . . .

EPILOGUE

An Interview With St. Peter — Sometime Later

All at once I wakened as from a deep sleep. There was a great light and a gate slid open, soundlessly, as if by some magic touch, and a patriarchal figure, benign as the white cloud behind him, stood before me.

"Oh," I said, stuttering, "are you, maybe you're, *could* you be St. Peter?" limp as a rag after getting it all out. He smiled and answered, "Of course, who else?" with a chuckle; and gently shunted me inside the Pearly Gates.

"Well, if you're St. Peter, this must be Heaven; but where *is* everybody? I can't see a soul?"

"That's just it," he answered, "and you've hit on the right word," knowingly shaking his head. "They're all here, trillions of them," pointing to a White Door beside him, "but you don't '*see*' souls, you '*feel*' them; and they have got to feel you too, or there's no contact."

"Oh," was all I could say to that.

Then, seeing the disappointed look on my face, he added, "But never mind, your two will 'feel' *you,* and they'll be here in a minute."

They came running, Glindy and Cerid, wonderful-looking and years younger in appearance. Cerid had her girlish figure back again, that she lost with the birthing of her babies, and she was beautiful. Glindy, speechless with emotion at the sight of me, was utterly handsome, too, and almost a dead-ringer for "Maracas Masterpiece," at one time the top corgi in Wales, and for that matter in the whole world, according to some authorities.

"*That* young fellow," said St. Peter, relishing my fond look at Glindy, "took a first at the Dog Show today, beating the *best* of them."

"Oh, do they have dog shows in *Heaven?*" I stammered incredulously, because it wasn't good news at all and I told St. Peter so — adding they were "trouble enough on earth, and expensive, too . . . *why* have them in Heaven?"

"Well, we have plenty of them," he commented, "but they're no great problem here because everybody wins, and no expense either, because everything's free up here in Heaven."

I stood there stupidly, like when a person says the wrong thing and doesn't know how to apologize.

Glindy and Cerid were paying no attention to St. Peter and me, but were rolling all over themselves and the floor, with glee. It was embarrassing, and St. Peter asked, "What's come over *those* two?" pointing to them.

They both stopped, and came straight to me, standing one on each side of me.

"Hmmmmm," so *that's* it," said St. Peter stroking his bearded chin, "they are getting impatient, and want to go in . . . well, you'd better go before they become rambunctious."

So saying, he turned to the Great White Door, and opened it just a little — enough for the three of us to squeeze in.

Immediately, there was a loud, exultant cry of "Hallelujah, Hallelujah." Tremendous! Magnificent!

"Oh, they're singing the Hallelujah Chorus," I shouted to Glindy and Cerid, "Let's join them — *we* know it!

The three of us added our voices to the others in a loud paean of praise and thanksgiving to God. Soon Glindy, and even Cerid, who had *never* sung a note of music in her *life,* were singing at the tops of their lungs, joyfully taking the lead, dwarfing the others and never missing a single "Hallelujah," until Handel's mighty chorus came to an end. . . .

Then a loud roar, like the roar of the sea, engulfed everything; everybody was laughing and applauding enthusiastically, as Glindy and Cerid finished singing. Shouts of "Bravo, *BRAVO!*" filled the air, and they all seemed wonderfully happy, not just with the sight and sound of two dogs singing, but with an inner joy, an inner peace, an inner reconciliation with everything and everybody, that included all of Nature and Humanity, no exceptions. . . .

It was beautiful to see *and* feel, this "universal" kinship with everything and everyone — this supreme affinity with the Creator and all things created. Glindy, Cerid and I became part of it, and "belonged." We revelled in it — and *rejoiced* — as St. Peter raised his right hand, and waved us through . . . to Eternity.

Esther Elias

Pittsburgh   THE END
Autumn, 1979